The
Mystery of the Holy Trinity in Oldest Judaism

BY

FRANK McGLOIN, LL. D.

KNIGHT OF ST. GREGORY

Author of "Norodom—King of Cambodia," "The Light of
Faith," "The Conquest of Europe," etc.

"Thy Kingdom Come"

PHILADELPHIA

JOHN JOSEPH McVEY

1916

Nihil Obstat:

N. F. FISHER, S. T. L.,
Censor Librorum.

Die 29 Februarii, 1916.

Imprimatur:

✠ EDMUNDUS FRANCISCUS,
Archiepiscopus Philadelphiensis.

Die 2 Martii, 1916.

TO MY BELOVED SISTER,

MADAME ELEONORE McGLOIN, R. S. H.,

IN GRATEFUL RECOGNITION OF HER VALUED ASSISTANCE

IN THE

PREPARATION AND PUBLICATION

OF THIS WORK.

CARDINAL'S RESIDENCE.

408 N. Charles St., Baltimore.

It is with great pleasure that I recommend to the public Dr. McGloin's masterly work entitled "The Mystery of the Trinity in Older Judaism," which is about to be published and which has obtained such strong commendation from the Most Reverend Archbishop of New Orleans. The work is, I am sure, destined to do a great deal of good, and Dr. McGloin is to be commended for the spirit of piety and zeal which has prompted its publication.

J. Card. Gibbons,
Archbishop of Baltimore.

FOREWORD.

THE Doctors and Fathers of the Church agree in recognizing that the august mystery of the Blessed Trinity is not found explicitly revealed in any of the pages of the Old Testament. This mystery is the supreme manifestation of God's most intimate life. To it, the entire Christian revelation converges, and the Divine Master seems to have reserved to Himself the privilege of teaching it to men in person, when He dwelt amongst them. With good reason, however, could St. Augustine say that "the Scriptures of the Old and the New Testament, if read with a true Christian spirit, testify that the Father, the Son and the Holy Ghost are one only God in the unity of essence and substance."

In fact, from the earliest dawn of man's existence, the Divine Goodness has deigned to manifest something of the splendor of this supreme and adorable mystery. On casting a glance over the majestic pages of Genesis, it seems impossible to resist the impression that, beneath a form of elocution strange to us, but easy and altogether sublime, there is hidden something mysterious pertaining to the essence and personality of that God, who reveals Himself to our astonished sense in the pronouncing of a *word*, which, resounding through the fathomless abysses of nothingness, calls forth into existence the heavens and the earth, and the whole creation, of which they form part.

By the side of this sovereign God who utters a word so mysterious, so all-potent, there also appears the Spirit of God, moving over the chaos of the waters, and manifesting Himself in the production therein of that magnificence of endless variety and all-pervading harmony in the immeasurable vastness of a Universe, which is still but a pale reflection of God's infinite power, wisdom and love.[1]

The Fathers and Doctors of the Church are also of one mind in seeing in the passage here referred to, and in others of the Old Testament, an intimation, an implicit revelation of the mystery of the Blessed Trinity, which the Savior deigned to reveal to us with such precision in the Gospel. Purposely, we refrain from a critical study of these passages, as it would lead us too far, and, besides, we would be only redoing the work so well done by Dr. McGloin.

St. Gregory the Great affirms distinctly that "the Patriarchs and Prophets of the Old Testament possessed a precise knowledge of the mystery of the Blessed Trinity, and an explicit faith in it, though they very prudently refrained from proclaiming it to the people.[2] The Angelic Doctor insists upon St. Gregory's teaching, and maintains that as without faith in the Savior, no one has ever attained eternal

---

[1] "Omnis Scriptura Veteris ac Novi Testamenti, si catholice intelligatur, hoc insinuat quod Pater, Filius et Spiritus Sanctus unus sint Deus, ejusdem essentiæ atque substantiæ." Sermo 3, Dom. infra oct. Epiphaniæ.

[2] "Sancti Patres quos per S. Scripturam ante Legem fuisse cognovimus, unum quidem omnipotentem Deum, sanctam videlicet Trinitatem esse noverunt, sed eamdem Trinitatem quam cognoverunt, minime predicaverunt." In Ezeq. lib. 2 hom. 16.

salvation, so neither has any one attained it without
faith in the Blessed Trinity, because faith in the
Savior is incomprehensible without a belief in the
Trinity of Persons. However, not all the Jews possessed the same degree of faith in the Savior. The
Patriarchs and Prophets upon whom fell the charge
of teaching the people, possessed a most lively faith
in the future Savior, and the happiness of their existence lay in the hope of His coming; but the rest
of the Jewish people did not profess so precise and
explicit faith in this mystery. Their faith, without
losing any of its supernatural value, seems to have
been enveloped in shadows more dense. The more
concrete and explicit formula by which they expressed their faith in this exalted mystery, was the
act of lending assent to all that God had deigned to
reveal concerning Man's redemption to the elders,
who were the custodians and teachers of religious
knowledge.

Owing to the intrinsic union existing between the
mystery of the Redemption and that of the Trinity
of Persons, St. Thomas extends to this second mystery the doctrine which he so conclusively established concerning the first. To him, the question of
the Blessed Trinity and that of the Redemption are,
in essence, identically the same. To ask whether the
ancient Jews knew the mystery of the Trinity and
had faith in it, is equivalent to asking if they knew
of the future Redeemer and had faith in Him. The
fact of their knowledge of the Redeemer and their
faith in Him once established, it must of necessity
be admitted that they were also acquainted with the

mystery of the Blessed Trinity and believed in it.[1]
Owing to the solid and incontrovertible arguments
of the Angelic Doctor, all theologians have been compelled to accept his teaching on this point. This
common opinion of Ecclesiastical Doctors has received additional light from the conscientious study
of Dr. McGloin, whom we have the honor of introducing to the learned public. A judicious and
searching criticism of the Scriptural texts and of
the traditions of the Jewish people bearing upon this
fundamental mystery of our Christian faith form
the content of the present work which, we doubt not,
will be received with applause, not only by men of
letters, but also by the faithful in general, because
for all it contains salutary teachings expressed with
a clearness of exposition and language that places
them within the reach of any mind of good average
culture. It is a valuable contribution to the Science
of Positive Theology or History of the Dogmas, as
it is termed in the present day.

Nor can it fail to be practically helpful to many
among those sincere seekers after religious truth
who, fortunately, are numerous enough among our
people, by clearing some, at least, of their difficulties
out of their way; while its very title must prove an
attraction for the educated class among our Jewish
fellow-citizens who are naturally interested in whatever reminds them of the ancient glories of their
race so favored of old by Jehovah.

[1] ". . . et ideo eodem mode quo mysterium Incarnationis
Christi ante Christum fuit explicite creditum a majoribus, im-
plicite et quasi obumbrate a minoribus, ita etiam et mysterium
Trinitatis. . . ." 2a-2æ quæst. LL art. 8.

We do not think it will be detracting from the merit of the present monograph to mention that, to some extent, he has made the studies of Dr. Drach [1] the starting point of his own, but not without carefully sifting his facts and conclusions, and bringing them out into stronger relief by the addition of new data and giving them also a new support by cogent arguments of his own.

From the reading of Dr. McGloin's work, we draw the following conclusions: 1st. The Patriarchs, Prophets and other great personages among the Jewish people had an explicit faith in the mystery of the Blessed Trinity. 2d. The Doctors of the Law, without arriving at so distinct a knowledge of the mystery as the Patriarchs and Prophets possessed, yet understood it with some clearness, as evidenced by Rabinnical literature. 3d. That the Jewish people in general had not an explicit knowledge of the blessed Trinity; for the great mass of them, in spite of their marked superiority over the pagan nations around them, had their share of the grossness of mind and customs prevailing everywhere in the ancient world, a grossness which Moses, their inspired Law-giver, had to take so largely into account in framing his code of legislation, and which caused them to lapse so often and so easily into idolatry. And, for this reason, apparently, the mystery of the Blessed Trinity, both in the Sacred Scriptures and in Rabbinical literature, was enveloped in the obscurity of symbolism.

We unhesitatingly believe the present work to be

[1] *De l'Harmonie entre l'Eglise et la Synagogue.*

a splendid contribution to theological studies, one that will hand the name of Dr. McGloin down to posterity, and make him figure worthily among those thinkers whose personal labors have contributed to build up the great edifice of religious science.

JAMES HUBERT BLENK, S. M.,
Archbishop of New Orleans.

NEW ORLEANS, 1915.
Feast of the Immaculate Conception.

CONTENTS.

	PAGE
CARDINAL'S LETTER	v
FOREWORD	vii
PREFACE.—Some Introductory Thoughts on the Holy Trinity	1

CHAPTER

I.—Were the Ancient Hebrews Unitarians?	17
II.—"In the Head of the Book"	33
III.—Elohim	52
IV.—"The Lord Said to My Lord."—Psalm 109 (110)	66
V.—"Hear, O Israel: The Lord, Our God, the Lord is ONE."—Deut. 6:4	86
VI.—"The Word of Jehova"	103
VII.—"Let Us Make Man."—Gen. 1:25	114
VIII.—Is Man to the Image of the Trinity?	128
IX.—"In the Vale of Mambre."—Genesis 18	140
X.—"The Angel of Jehova"	154
XI.—The Spirit of God	168
XII.—The Ineffable Name—Jehova	182
XIII.—The Letter Schin, on the Jewish Phylacteries	206
XIV.—The Songs of the Degrees	218

xiii

PREFACE.

Some Introductory Thoughts on the Holy Trinity.

1. We owe our knowledge of the dogma of the Holy Trinity solely to supernatural revelation. Natural reason [1] alone would not have disclosed it to us; and, in the visible works of the Almighty, there is nothing which manifests it.

2. The impartial mind sees in the universe evidence of God's existence, of His Eternity, of His infinite power, wisdom, goodness, etc. But there is a limit to what nature alone can tell us, with regard to the Creator. It conveys no lesson as to God's ultimate substance, essence or nature; it cannot explain the mystery of God's eternal self-existence, or show how He has made something out of nothing.

3. However, though the external Universe be mute, and our own reason unresponsive concerning the ultimate nature of God, there is, on the other hand, nothing in visible creation, or in human consciousness or thought, to disprove the Trinity. Our understanding, once informed, is unable to advance any valid reason why the One and Only God should not be in three divine Persons as well as in one.

---

[1] By "natural reason" here we mean the wise discernment, or insight of the human intellect, exerting its own powers, and without immediate illumination or assistance from God. It is, for instance, natural reason, aided by observation, which has developed the secular sciences, as we have them now: Astronomy, Biology, Chemistry, etc.

1

4.   We know little, in any direction, concerning ultimates.   It is conceded that, in the study of physics, every avenue of investigation leads sooner or later to mystery.[1] But, to God, everything is open and known; and no man can say that the divine disposition, as to these greater and deeper things, or matters, are or must be against reason, simply because of his inability to solve final problems unaided.

5.   The wiser and only practical course for Christians, with regard to the dogma of the Holy Trinity, is to accept it, without doubt or hesitation, and on the strength of Revelation.   We believe in God, and in Revelation.   We accept this dogma as a part of the divine revelation.   This is enough to logically justify us in the conviction that God is triune.   And our attitude should be the same, even did our human understandings find some seemingly valid ground for rebelling against the concept now in question, as involving an apparent impossibility; for, after all, human reason has its limitations, and its judgments, even as to material things, and as to physical conditions, are often deceptive.[2]

[1] "I compare the mind of man to a musical instrument, with a certain range of notes, beyond which, in both directions, exists infinite silence.   The phenomena of matter and force come within our intellectual range; but behind and above and around us the real mystery of the Universe lies unsolved, and, so far as we are concerned is incapable of solution." Tyndall, *Fragments of Science,* Vol. II, Chap. 15, p. 393; Appleton. Revelation, of course, from the standpoint of Christian teaching, greatly extends the range of human knowledge in some directions, yet still beyond all our powers, even as thus assisted, the abysses of mystery remain outspread indefinitely.

[2] "It is not surprising that the naturalists of the early part of the present century could not believe in the existence of a

6.   When a man challenges our faith in the Trinity, we are entitled to know of him whether he himself believes in God and in Revelation. If he professes disbelief even in the being of God, it is useless to attempt discussing with him concerning the nature of God, and if he rejects all revelation, it is mere waste of time to debate with him over the teachings of Holy Writ.

7.   Some there are, claiming to be Christians, who will not accept this great dogma, asserting that the thought involved is logically impossible. They pretend that proclaiming three divine Persons, each possessed of all the divine attributes in their fullness, is really to stand for three separate and distinct Gods and not for one only. And, they contend further that personality necessarily involves individuality, and that every individual, to be such, must differ in something from all his fellows, must possess something which the latter have not. This thought, it is urged, is not compatible with that of an infinite divine perfection, for, they say, if the Father possesses some particular thing which the Son and the Holy Ghost have not, and the possession of which differentiates the First Person of the Trinity from

fauna at the bottom of the deep seas. The extraordinary conditions of such a region—the enormous pressure, the absolute darkness, the probable absence of any vegetable life from want of direct sunlight—might very well have been considered sufficient to form an impassible barrier to the animals migrating from the shallow waters and to prevent the development of fauna particularly its own." Hickson, *Fauna of the Deep Sea,* Chap. 2, p. 17, D. Appleton & Co. We remember how, some years ago, it was argued by some that there could be no resurrection of the body, because grass grew on the graves of the dead, and goats eat the grass.

the Second and Third, then the Son and the Holy Ghost must be correspondingly deficient and less than perfect.

8. Such lines of argument are based upon two assumptions, neither of which can be granted. The first is that invisible nature must of necessity be, in all respects, like the visible; that all spiritual and higher being, including that of the Almighty God Himself, must be, in substance and nature, precisely what our own human being is. The second assumption is that, by its own unaided efforts, the human mind may plunge succcessfully into the abysses of the divine infinitude and fully acquaint itself with the very ultimate nature of the Almighty Himself.

9. Could reason suddenly be given to the stones upon some dead planet in space, would not these stones, with their limited lights and scant experience, discredit the statement that, upon other orbs, there are beings which manifest those wonderful phenomena which, as our own human experience teaches us always accompany on earth the presence of natural life? Would they not argue thus: "We stones, in our entireties and in all our parts are inert and stationary; we are not perpetually changing the matter of which we are composed.[1] We are not

---

[1] "The chemist equally regards chemical change in a body as the effect of the action of something external to the body changed. A chemical compound once formed would persist forever if no alteration took place in surrounding conditions.

"But to the student of life, the aspect of nature is reversed. Here, incessant, and, so far as we know, spontaneous change is the rule, rest the exception—the anomaly to be accounted for. Living things have no inertia and tend to no equilibrium." Huxley, *Lay Sermons,* Serm. 5, p. 73.

taking in new material from the outside, transforming it into living parts of ourselves and restoring it again, after a time, dead to the external world.[1] We do not reproduce our kind."

10. But, despite such a reasoning from the stones, the fact would remain that in the world of animate being as it shows itself to us on earth, all of the wonderful phenomena of life are to be seen. The lesson from this in the present connection, is that, as the nature and constitution of inanimate things afford no rule by which to determine the possibilities and impossibilities of animate nature, so the nature and constitution of man do not necessarily indicate the nature and substance of God.

11. As for the inability of the human intellect to fathom, unaided, the profounder mysteries of being, or to speak with authority concerning the ultimate nature of things, we are not compelled, in proof of the statement, to rise up so high as the Deity Itself. The very material Universe, of which we form a part is, to a great extent, a sealed book to us. We live, surrounded by mysteries, the solving of which is beyond our mental powers. What, finally, is matter?

[1] "Just as the flame remains the same in appearance, and continues to exist with the same form and structure, although it draws every minute fresh combustible vapor, and fresh oxygen from the air into the vortex of its ascending current; and just as the wave goes on in unaltered form, and is yet being reconstructed every moment from fresh particles of water, so also, in the living being, it is not the definite mass of substance, which now constitutes the body, to which the continuance of the individual is attached. For the material body, like that of the flame is subject to continuous and comparatively rapid change—a change the more rapid, the livelier the activity of the organs in question." Helmholtz, *Popular Lectures*, Lect. 4, p. 195.

What is force? What is life? What is consciousness? [1]

12. These questions, and a number of others,
equally unanswerable arise perpetually to humble
the human intellect.

These numerous enigmas, with which the visible
Universe confronts us, are such to us, because of the
incapacity of our minds to deal with them. We cannot in any of these different cases, judge of what lies
behind the veil, simply and solely from the study of
what we can see before it.

13. If this be so, with regard to the principles of
all the mere works of God, how much more so must it
be with regard to the ultimate substance and nature
of God Himself, Who holds the whole Universe in
the palm of His hand, and Who, beyond all the things
He Himself had made, must be the Mystery of Mysteries? And, if it be true that the Almighty has revealed that He Himself is in fact Triune, shall His
divine word be contradicted, for no other reason than

[1] "This objection is quite correct, but it applies equally to
all explanations of phenomena. We nowhere arrive at a knowledge of first causes. The origin of every simple salt crystal,
which we obtain by evaporating its mother-liquor, is no less
mysterious to us, as far as concerns its first cause, and is itself
no less incomprehensible than the origin of every animal which
is developed out of a simple cell. In explaining the most
simple physical or chemical phenomena, as the falling of a
stone, or the formation of a chemical combination, we arrive,
by discovering and establishing the active causes—for example,
the gravitation or the chemical affinity—at other remoter phenomena, which in themselves are mysterious. This arises from
the limitation or relativity of our powers of understanding.
We must not forget that human knowledge is absolutely limited and possesses only a relative extension. It is in its essence, limited by the very nature of our senses and of our
brains." Hæckel, *History of Creation,* Vol. I, Chap. 2, p. 31.

that a man or an animal, a plant or a stone cannot similarly exist three in one? [1]

14.   Experience with sensible objects proves to us that they are all of them subjected to certain natural laws, and limited in many ways.   And some thinkers are inclined to believe that no existence of any sort is possible, free from subjection to physical law and from the limitations which affect material objects; but this is a *non sequitur.*

15.   No man or animal can pass through an unbroken wall of steel, but this does not prove that a similar barrier could stop the progress of a pure spirit.   Only one man at a time can stand on one and the same spot of ground, nevertheless, it may well be that a thousand angels might occupy simultaneously the very same part or portion of space.   The human being, body and soul, cannot be, naturally, in two places at one and the same time, yet we have about us visible evidences of the presence of God everywhere, throughout the realms of space.[2]

[1] The acorn is small, yet in some incomprehensible way, it contains within itself, potentially, the majestic oak, with its massive trunk, its spread of roots, its mass of foliage.   And, with time, that oak will bring forth successive crops of new acorns.   So, it may be truly said that, within the tiny shell of the parent acorn were present, potentially, tens of thousands of other acorns.   Were it not that our own constant, personal observation compels us to recognize the mysterious actuality, would we mortals be content to accept, as credible, the story of the acorn?

[2] "In yon gilded canopy of heaven we see the broad aspect of the Universe, where each shining point presents us with a sun, and each sun with a system of worlds; where the Divinity reigns in all the grandeur of His attributes; where He peoples immensity with His wonders, and travels in the greatness of His strength through the dominions of one vast and unlimited monarchy."   Chalmers, *Astronomical Discourses,* p. 31.

16.   Those who seem convinced that the divine nature must be subjected to the same conditions and limitations as are imposed upon the human, must find, as they meditate upon the Deity, that their theory is antagonized by other attributes or characteristics of God, besides the one of His triune being. How, for instance, are we to conform the thoughts of the divine omnipresence and of the divine infinitude generally with our own actual experience as to personality or individuality, according to human conditions, which shows always differentiation and therefore limitation and unidentity.

17.   All objections, based upon these assumptions, are equally futile, since there is no warrant for the belief that all the conditions of the seen world must be conditions, also of the unseen.   Even as to our own human nature, the limitations to which we have just referred, as we see and know these limitations, attach to our material part, the body.   Were our souls with their powers of feeling and thinking and exercising will and memory freed from the prison house of the flesh, they would, at the same time, escape from many of the conditions which hamper and restrain us in this life, and which by some are wrongly considered as necessary features of all existence.   And if, in dealing even with the lesser and created spiritual beings, we should leave out of consideration the conditions and limitations which attach to all corporeity, how much more necessary is it to exclude such elements, when we meditate upon the nature of the One, Omnipotent, and Eternal God.

18.   What, after all, is a "person"?   Bœthius tells

us that a "person" is "an individual substance of a rational nature;" and this definition has been approved by many philosophers. The ruling thought in this definition is set out in the words "of a rational nature."

19. Only the Atheist, and his twin brother, the Pantheist, pretend that there is no true difference between a rational nature and a material one.[1] Experience teaches us that there are about us millions

---

[1] According to Pantheism, distinct as objects may seem to be each from the others, there is actually no difference anywhere, or between any things. Spirit and matter are not two independent orders of being, but, in their final analysis, are one and the same. There is throughout all space but one general substance, one universal nature. As the material world is restless and ever changing, so the God of the Pantheist must be conceived as also variable, constantly new—forming in places and parts and dissolving in other places and parts. In order to conform to this notion, we should conceive the material universe to be infinitely extended, and matter to be as it were omnipresent; otherwise God would be not infinite in extent but limited, and there would be places where He is not. If men be not, each one of them, a particular or individual being, but are so many parts only of a Pantheistic God, then every human act committed or done has been the act of God. Consequently, all of the black crimes perpetrated since the dawn of time are God's crimes, and every abomination, supposed to have been human, is in fact divine. All this matter is not outside of the pale of our observation, or beyond the reach of our reason. Our senses can and do inform us that this Universe is made up of a vast number of distinct entities, persons and things; and such is the general conclusion of all mankind. Furthermore, the consciousness of every man declares to him that he himself is a particular individual or person, feeling, thinking and acting by and for himself, and not confused in any way with the other and exterior beings, whether similar to himself, or dissimilar, by which he is surrounded. When a man is willing to dispute the long continued evidence of the human senses, to ignore the universal verdict of humanity, and to falsify the testimony of his own consciousness, then is he fitted to present himself to the world as a Pantheist.

of objects which are of a strictly material nature, having no trace of consciousness or reason. The physical death which awaits us all affords us here a striking illustration. While we live, intellect exists within us and does its noble work: when we are dead, all is stilled, and on earth, there is nothing left of us but dust.

20.   Inanimate things are not "persons." No one dreams of classing sticks or stones as such. A living man is a "person," but a corpse is not. Furthermore, it is true reason or understanding that constitutes the "rational nature," which marks the "person." The instinct, or the faint glimmer of intelligence, if so we prefer to regard it, which belongs to brutes is different in its nature from real understanding; and in any view, it is so infinitesimal as to require the neglecting of it entirely, in this connection. Therefore it is that men do not speak of horses, dogs, etc., as "persons."

21.   It follows, from what has been said that any being having and exercising true reason or understanding is a "person"; and to deny the personality of God is to deny that God has and exercises understanding. The same universe, which is about us, and which, by its immensity, its complexity, its harmony and balance, etc., serves to demonstrate God's existence, demonstrates also His infinite intelligence and shows His divine personality. And he who questions the personality of God must, in defending his theory, disregard the same patent proofs, which Atheists and Agnostics also profess to ignore, and for the same reasons.

22. The nature of God's substance is, of course, an unfathomable mystery to us: it is a something which is infinitely beyond the reach of our finite understandings. But this intellectual inability on our part does not militate against either of the great associated facts just referred to, and which we cannot but perceive; that is, the *existence* of the One, Omnipresent, All-wise and Eternal God and His *personality.*

23. The thought of God's Omnipresence harmonizes perfectly with that of His Personality. Difficulties, in this connection, disappear, we think, or are minimized, when we come to a truer understanding of the words which, in such a study as this, we are compelled to use. Omnipresence, here, is not the equivalent of ubiquity or of mere everywhereness. The ether probably is everywhere through space; and the atmosphere is everywhere above and over our earth. But, in neither of these cases have we that true Omnipresence, which is God's mode of being. The divine Omnipresence is more than mere physical contact, or pervasion or permeation. The ether is not all of it present in or about our sun; the atmosphere is not all of it in or over the City of New York. On the other hand, God can be and is omnipresent in the fullest meaning of the term; that is, He is actually present in every spot and place, in the very fullness of His being and nature. It is not, therefore, one part or portion of God, which is in Europe and another part or portion which is in America; the Almighty is simultaneously and ever present, in the fullness of His nature, in and upon

every continent and ocean of this earth, and in and
upon every planet and star, and in and through every
point of intervening space.

24.   Our human understanding cannot reach fully
up to these sublime levels of contemplation, but this
should not prevent us from recognizing that there is
no choice between Atheism or Agnosticism on the one
hand, and the acknowledgment of God's Omnipresence on the other.   Let us suppose an Architect and
Builder, who is constructing some great edifice.   In
such a case, not only the general design or plan must
be drawn by him, but every detail also, from top to
bottom and from beginning to end, must bear the im-
press of his genius and must receive his care and
attention.

25.   As things are with us upon earth, the Architect supposed would be compelled to multiply himself, as it were, by engaging a great number of
trained asistants, each one of whom would be required to put into effect, by his own wisdom and
skill, in some particular place or places, the designs
of the master.   All the same, although every different operation, in the progress of the building, would
demand the use of human intelligence, it would still
be the will, or wishes of the Architect which were being put into execution: and he would be thus present
everywhere over the work, either in person or by
representation.

26.   Were such a constructor infinitely wise and
also omnipotent, he could himself alone accomplish
the entire work, which he had designed.   But, as
every detail requires application of intelligence and

skill for its working out, he would have to give his own attention and thought to every single act or operation from beginning to end; and, therefore, he would be present designing and executing in all parts at one and the same time. In other words, the omnipresence which, under the conditions first supposed, was personal and by representation, under those last suggested would be exclusively personal.

27. God is the universal and sole Creator. He has made the outermost star in all space, just as he has made this earth upon which we live. The forming of the one out of nothing is as incomprehensible as the similar formation of the other; and in each case the divine wisdom and the divine omnipotence were both needed, present and operating. Therefore, when God created, for instance, the great Arcturus, He was there present in His infinite wisdom and in His Omnipotence; and, as our own sun and its planets probably came into being simultaneously with Arcturus, God, at the same time was similarly present here, exercising His Wisdom and Power. And it was the same with the uncounted millions of other suns which inhabit space; each one of the numberless multitude is an immense and contemporaneous effect of the Wisdom and the Will of God.[1] And then this vast number of great suns are

[1] "Now light takes more than eight minutes in reaching us from the sun, whose distance is more than 91,000,000 of miles; and it is easily calculated that the long journey from Sirius cannot be in less than fifteen years. More probably it requires more than twenty years; and the greater number of the stars we see on a dark and clear night lie much further away than Sirius. Some of them certainly lie at distances which light can only traverse in hundreds of years. So soon as we

bound together, throughout the extent of space; and all alike are governed and controlled and preserved. God is present to the inhabitants, if any, of the most distant systems, just as He is present with us on earth; present everywhere in the fullness of His majesty, power and wisdom, and in the exercise of His merciful Providence.[1]   Similarly, He is present on earth, with the solitary Arab who spurs his steed over the sands of the Sahara, the same as with the busy merchant in his counting room in the great City of London.

28.   The belief in Polytheism is confined in this day to barbarians of degraded type. The evidences of unity of plan and unity in methods of work throughout the universe are now too numerous and too convincing to justify any wise man in supposing it the joint result of the efforts of a number of petty deities.   The same elements, or components, are

turn, however, to telescopic stars, the range of time over which our vision extends is enormously increased, and it is certainly not too much to say that some of the fainter stars revealed by the great Rosse telescope lie at distances so enormous that their light has taken more than a hundred thousand years in reaching us. Then beyond these stars lie millions and millions of orbs yet further away. There is no limit to the range of space occupied thus with the work of God's hands. All that has been taught us by Astronomy suggests the lesson that every moment light reaches the earth from unseen orbs so far away that the journey over the vast abysses separating us from them has not been completed in less than millions of years." Proctor's *Expanse of the Heavens,* p. 202.

[1] We might descend into the realm of the minute, and study here, with profit, the nature of the molecule and of the atom, according to generally accepted scientific theories. We there would learn more clearly the lesson of the unity of all creation, and we would see in every such single molecule and in every atom, the same as in the greatest of stars, evidence of God's presence and of His power.

found entering into the formation of stars which are separated from each other by immense distances. Gravitation is an invisible chain which binds together in one immense system, all the suns, with their attendants, which are scattered so widely and far throughout space. And each of the innumerable orbs which are speeding through its abysses, sends forth its flood of light, to reach in time its far-off sister stars. Therefore there is left to the instructed man no choice except to confess the one eternal and Omnipresent God, or to senselessly deny Him, positively as the Atheist does, or by inference like the Agnostic.

29. If we must recognize the Omnipresence of God, by the simultaneous operation everywhere of His Wisdom and Power; and if the definition of Bœthius for the word "person," as already referred to above, is to be accepted as substantially correct, must not the same divine Wisdom and the same divine Will, operating thus together, in all places and shaping and moulding all things, show God to be of an understanding nature and therefore a person?

30. If this definition of Bœthius be unsatisfactory to any one for present purposes, let those who are disposed to reject it, furnish a better. And if there be any sufficient warrant for certainly concluding that, because in a finite man there cannot exist three persons in one essence or substance,[1] therefore

---

[1] In man we have not three persons in one being, but we have two natures in one person: corporal and spiritual. One nature man shares with the brutes, the other with God and the Angels. And the Savior of Mankind has the two natures, divine and human, hypostatically united in the Person of Christ. Mysteries both of these, beyond our understanding, yet we believe in them.

the Eternal and Omnipotent God must be equally as incapable of so existing, let those who so think point out in what this warrant consists.

31.   For the reasons considered above, the question of revelation assumes in this study the position of prime importance. If God Himself has said to man that the divine nature is Triune, those who venture to dispute such a divine announcement simply because in the realm of matter, or in that of the psycho-material, such a mode of being has never been found, merit condemnation, for they give the lie to God. The aim of this volume is to establish by a multitude of different proofs, taken from the Old Testament principally, and also from the Rabbinical Commentaries upon it, that the Ancient Hebrews knew of the dogma of the Holy Trinity and accepted it.

32.   The soundness of this conclusion depends not upon any one particular argument, or upon any one particular line of arguments, that may be presented in its defense. It rests upon an entire array of substantial proofs.

33.   It is not to be expected that any book, whose subject is so difficult as the one dealt with herein, should show itself, in all respect and parts, beyond just criticism and free from all need of correction. But the possible discrediting of any part or parts of this present work cannot destroy the probative force of its other parts, or minimize the effect, in this connection, of the unmistakable fact, that this great dogma of the Holy Trinity is a key that serves to solve very many of the problems which confront every thoughtful student of our sacred literature.

CHAPTER I.

WERE THE ANCIENT HEBREWS UNITARIANS?

34. THE two great truths of the Trinity and of the Divinity of Jesus Christ are so closely united as, for purposes of discussion, to constitute practically one. If there be not a plurality of persons in God, there can be, of course, no Divine Messiah. Therefore, the reasons which go to show that the Holy Trinity exists are reasons, also, in favor of belief in the deity of Our Blessed Redeemer: and all that tends to demonstrate the Divine Nature of the Son of God is proof as well of the existence of the Father and of the Holy Ghost.

35. Enemies of our Christian Faith assert that belief in the Holy Trinity is of modern origin; that, consequently, it was unknown to the Ancient Hebrews. Their further contention necessarily is that the doctrine of the divinity of Christ is likewise an invention of later days.

36. The question thus presented, though apparently single, at first sight, is in reality double. Whether or not the sacred dogmas, which we are now considering were known in any shape or form to the Jews of old is one subject of inquiry, and whether they are to be found formally disclosed in the Old Testament is another.

37. These are important issues of fact, calling each for a separate study. Therefore, we shall con-

fine ourselves in this chapter to the consideration of the first.

38. Even if it be conceded for argument's sake, that the inspired writers, before the time of Christ, were utterly silent with regard to the Holy Trinity and the Divinity of the expected Messiah, the second question must still present itself, whether the Sacred Writings of the Old Dispensation contain the whole of the Revelation, delivered to the Ancient Hebrews. The text of Sacred Writ is not, after all, so ample, nor its narrative so full and continuous, nor the exposition of its doctrine so methodical and complete, nor its expressions always so free from obscurity, as to warrant the conclusion, based solely upon the appearance and construction of its several books, that it constituted alone the entire body of divine law given to Israel before the Advent of Christ.

39. The objection sometimes made to the Older Scriptures that they seem in places broken and obscure, may or may not have a certain force in face of the contention that these venerable writings contain all, in the nature of divine revelation, that was ever given to the Jewish Nation. But it fails entirely as against the proposition that, outside of the Ten Commandments, the original deposit of divine faith and law was oral, and that the reduction to writing of any portion of that original oral deposit was for the purpose only of serving as a help in the task of preserving that deposit true and unaltered, and assisting in its correct interpretation.[1]

---

[1] The modern Rabbinical writers were cognizant of the true relation, or the interdependence rather, between the oral and

40. The arguments from necessity and from the experience of mankind are not available in support of the theory that the Old Testament contains all of the divine law which was known in Ancient Judea. No convincing reason can be advanced to prove that it was absolutely essential that Moses should have written down for his people every word that came from the Lord to him on Sinai. As for the testimony of human experience on this subject, it is a historical fact that many nations, especially in the earlier ages, were governed during generations by systems of law which were in greater part, and in some cases entirely consuetudinary. In England, for example, during a long period, civil affairs were regulated almost exclusively by the established usages of the realm; and even in our day the common law, *"lex non scripta,"* as Blackstone calls it, plays still an important part in the civil government of that country.

41. It seems manifest, therefore, that this question is strictly historical, in the sense that we may enter upon it with free minds and depend for the forming of our conclusions with regard to it, upon the historical evidence which is available.

42. Holy Scripture tells us that when Moses was

written law, received from God by Moses for his people, as may be seen by reference to note 14 to page 8, Vol. I, of Abbe L. Chiarini's *Translation of the Babylonian Talmud,* which note is as follows: "R. Josua Hallevit, Author of *Halicoth Olam or Key to the Talmud,* gives the reason that the written law contains mysteries in letters, which would perish if confided exclusively to tradition, and that the traditional law would become doubtful and subjected to discussions, if it were couched only in writing."

called by God upon Sinai to receive the law, he remained upon the mountain in conference with the Almighty during forty days and forty nights. Exod. 24:18; Deut. 9:9. Much must have been communicated to him by the Lord during that prolonged interval; and all that was given to him in written or graven form were the ten commandments.

43. It is true that the great Hebrew Lawgiver reduced to writing, from time to time, much of the revelation which had been given to him; but nothing appears in Holy Scripture to the effect that, even up to the date of his death, he had committed to paper the entire law. It is, however, declared that, immediately after coming down from Sinai, he communicated orally to his people all that he had heard from the Lord on the sacred summit. "And all the children of Israel came to him: and he gave them in commandment all that he had heard of the Lord on Mount Sinai. And, having done *speaking*, he put a veil upon his face." Exod. 34:32, 33. From this it may be inferred that, though Moses recognized the necessity of at once confiding to the nation the whole body of the law, he did not deem it essential or obligatory that he should place at once this same law in its entirety upon paper. It is certain, also, that at the outset, and during a period more or less prolonged, the revelation of Sinai existed almost wholly in oral form; and, as from time to time Moses for special purposes reduced parts thereof to writing, the Olden Hebrew law became more and more one written in part and in part traditional. A condition, which is thus shown to have existed during a

certain number of years, cannot have been intrinsically against right; and its persistence may be presumed in default of any express and positive showing to the contrary.

44. The reduction to statute form of any portion of a particular body of laws which had been previously consuetudinary or traditional, does not justify the inference that a complete abolition of all traditional law was either intended or effected by such action. In England, despite the fact that succeeding Parliaments have passed a multitude of statutes, there remains still in force a part of the Old Common Law of the Kingdom.

45. There is much historical authority in support of this theory that, all along under the Old Dispensation, a portion of the divine revelation made to Moses remained always oral, and was preserved in this shape and handed down from generation to generation of Jewish elders. We must look to Hebrew sources for information on this subject, for it could not be expected that either the chronicles or the traditions of other nations would cast much light upon such a subject. The Old Testament is the most ancient Hebrew history that we have, and its pages afford some evidence in favor of the theory we are considering. In Numbers, Chap. 11, verses 16, 17, we are told that God commanded Moses to gather together seventy of the ancients and masters of the people, who were to stand with him at the door of the tabernacle of the covenant and bear with him the burthen of the people. And these seventy chosen ones were to be endowed with the "Spirit of Moses"; that

is, with his wisdom and knowledge and inspiration. "And I will take of thy spirit and give to them." There is reason for believing that this body, thus established, persisted in some shape or other, from the time of the Exodus to that of Christ, as the recognized guardians and interpreters of the law, which had been first given to Moses.

46.   The Old Testament furnishes us with further proofs along the same line. In Deuteronomy, Chap. 32, verse 7, it is written: "Remember the days of old: think upon every generation: ask thy father and he will declare to thee: thy elders and they will tell thee." Baldad the Suhite advised Job to "enquire of the former generation, and search diligently into the memory of the fathers." Job 8:8. The prophet Jeremias enjoined upon his hearers to "Ask for the old paths, which is the good way and walk ye in it." Jere. 6:16. Aggeus, or Haggai 2:12 (11), *et seq.*, says: "Thus saith the Lord of Hosts: Ask the priests the law," etc. As corroborative of the foregoing, the following passages may also be consulted: Exod. 18:15, *et seq.*; Deut. 17:8, *et seq.*; Josue 4:6, 21; Job 15:18.

47.   Flavius Josephus, the great Jewish historian, born only a few years after the crucifixion (A. D. 37 or 38) is a witness, also, to the existence of an oral law in Judea, which had come down to his own generation from remote antiquity. He declares (Antiq., III, Chap. 5, No. 6) that Moses, after having made known to the people the commands of God, prescribed on subsequent occasions the manner in which, under those laws, they should act in all cases. In

Antiq. Book XIII, Chap. 10, No. 6, he further declares that the Pharisees gave to the people religious instruction which did not form part of the laws (written) of Moses, but which had come down to them by a continuous tradition from the ancestors of the nation. The Aramaic or Chaldee Paraphrases of Holy Scripture, which are known as the Targums and which are very ancient, mention the oral law in several places and contain moreover a number of traditions, some explaining the sense of the written law and others laying down precepts which are not found in the Pentateuch.[1]

48. The earlier records of Christianity, including the New Testament and the writings of the Older Church fathers, are also entitled to consideration in this connection. Christians will, of course, rank highest of all, the testimony of Our Lord Jesus Christ on any point or question upon which He has spoken. And even non-Christians, if at all fair-minded and informed, must regard the Gospels as historial documents of great authority and entitled to credit, when they deal with the customs and beliefs prevailing among the Jewish people at the opening of our Modern Era.

49. We have in this case evidence bearing upon our very question and coming from the Blessed Redeemer, Himself. The Gospel, according to Saint Matthew, Chap. 23, verses 1, 2, 3, is as follows: "Then Jesus spoke to the multitude and to his disciples saying: The Scribes and Pharisees have sitten

---

[1] Chevalier P. B. L. Drach, *De l'Harmonie entre l'Eglise et la Synagogue,* Vol. I, p. 128.

in the chair of Moses.   All, therefore, whatsoever, that they shall say to you, observe and do: but according to their works do ye not: for they say and do not."   Some English translations render by "sit in the chair of Moses," the corresponding words above quoted, but it is evident that the two forms express precisely the same meaning.   Sitting in the chair of Moses signified that the Scribes and Pharisees were in some way successors to the great lawgiver; that his office and authority had come down to them.   In the same way, somewhat, our own American President may now be spoken of as sitting in the chair of Washington.

50.   We have seen above that God gave to the seventy ancients, who were chosen to participate in the ruling of Israel, Num. 11:16, 17, the "Spirit" which had been given to Moses: "And I will take of thy spirit and give to them."   The Spirit of God resting thus in or with Moses was to keep faithfully in his mind the word of God which he had received for his people and to inspire him to correctly render and apply the divine revelation and law as occasion required.   And the Scribes and Pharisees, of the Savior's day, when sitting in the chair of Moses (that is, speaking in Sanhedrin assembled and officially; in other words, ex cathedra), had with them, for the purpose of guiding them in the correct rendition and application of the divine law, the same "Spirit of God," which had been imparted, as Holy Writ declares, from Moses to his Council of Seventy Elders.   It was for this reason that the official words of the Scribes and Pharisees, sitting in the

chair of Moses, were necessarily good and true to such an extent that Christ could command universal obedience to them, while their conduct was so wicked that the people were solemnly warned not to imitate it.

51. It is true that Christ, Himself, strongly denounced certain spurious traditions which had been imposed on the Jewish people by these same Scribes and Pharisees, styling them "the doctrines and precepts of men." Mark 7:3 to 13. But the Savior addressing some of these same Scribes and Pharisees on this subject, speaks of certain requirements they had imposed upon the nation as being the "traditions of men" and again as "your own tradition." Furthermore He charges against them that they were "making void *the word of God* by your tradition, which you have given forth."

52. We are permitted to conclude here, considering together, as we should, all that our Blessed Redeemer has said on this subject, that He did not on this occasion denounce sweepingly all tradition, but confined Himself to condemnation of the "traditions of men." There must have been other traditions which were not to be impugned, because of their being originally from God. We may consider that, when the Lord Jesus spoke here reprovingly of "your own traditions" it was to distinguish from the true traditions those false ones, which these men had themselves, and on their own authority "given forth" and which had not come to them by transmission from Moses.

53. That there were, at the beginning of our

Christian Era, certain religious traditions, fully accredited by the most enlightened among the Jews, is further established by the testimony of St. Paul. "And I made progress," he tells us, "in the Jews' religion above many of my equals in my own nation, being more abundantly zealous for the traditions of my fathers." Gal. 1:14. From this passage we may infer that "the progress in the Jews' religion," which the Apostle made as he informs us "above many of my equals in my own nation" consisted to a large extent in making himself more fully acquainted with these authentic traditions: for he ascribes his great progress to the fact that he was "more abundantly zealous for the traditions of my fathers." These "traditions of my fathers" are not condemned by St. Paul in any way; and the fact that he uses the restrictive clause "of my fathers" may be regarded as implying that there were also current at the time other traditions which were spurious because not genuine and truly ancestral. Indeed, from the very words of the text, we may justly conclude that, according to this testimony of St. Paul, "the Jews' religion" and "the traditions of my fathers" were to a great extent one and the same thing.

54. The early Church Fathers, who were so much nearer than we are to the sources of information on subjects of this character and who had access, no doubt, to literature dealing with this particular topic which is since lost, make plain mention of this oral law among the Jews. Saint Hilary, Bishop of Poitiers, for example, is very clear upon

this point.   And it will be observed that, in interpreting, as has been done above, the words of the Savior, in this regard, which have been already quoted, Matt. 23:1, 2, 3, we are but following in the wake of Church Fathers.   The great Bishop of Poitiers, on this point, speaks thus: "Besides the written law, Moses taught separately the most secret mysteries of the law to the Seventy Ancients, appointed in the capacity of Doctors in the Synagogue, especially charged to transmit its knowledge.   It is of this same traditional doctrine that Jesus Christ spoke when he said: 'the Scribes and Pharisees have sitten in the chair of Moses.   All, therefore, that they shall say to you observe and do, but according to their works do ye not.' "   Tract. in II Ps., Benedictine Edition, p. 28.

55.   The Talmud, which has ruled almost the entire Jewish race in its final dispersion during more than a thousand years, and which is even in our own day respected and obeyed by the majority of the children of Israel, depended for its authority upon the very same theory, which had been, as Josephus tells us, upheld by the Pharisees before the time of Christ.   When practically an entire nation is found to have so long respected and obeyed a system of law, originally at least in part written and in part oral, a fair presumption arises in favor of the antiquity and primal legitimacy of the system: and those who maintain that it was not primordial, that it was at some later time substituted for, or engrafted upon another and a conflicting system, have the burthen upon them of showing when and where and by whom the imposition was inaugurated,

Needless to say that, if the Hebrew people have been thus universally and lastingly deceived in a matter of such universal concern among themselves, no one has been able to designate with any show of certainty or authority at what time and by whom was caused or begun the general landslide of public opinion among the Jews, which thus dislodged the entire nation from an original conviction that all of the divine law was written, and planted them firmly and enduringly upon the theory that the original deposit of the faith and religious government, received and transmitted by Moses, was oral as well as written.

56. With regard to the Talmud, it is true that it abounds with most extravagant recitals, and that in parts it must be considered as positively indecent, but this does not destroy its value as aiding to establish the general proposition that the Jewish Nation always acknowledged and held that Moses had left an oral or traditional law with the written. This work was not begun, or at least was not reduced in any part to writing, until after the Crucifixion of the Savior and the subsequent final dispersion of the Jews; until after the Old Dispensation had given place in the providence of God to the New, and until the seat of Moses having been transferred to the Church of Christ, the Scribes and Pharisees could no longer sit therein. Having no longer the divine guidance and protection in the interpretation of the Law of Moses, they naturally wandered in many respects far away from truth; but despite this fact their writings retain some worth as corroborative proof of the conditions prevailing in this particular regard among

their remoter ancestors. The maxim *falsus in uno, falsus in omnibus* has a particular usefulness in dealing with the declaration of witnesses, testifying in judicial contests; but it would play havoc, if rigidly applied in the pursuit of general historical knowledge.

57. The conviction of the Jewish Rabbis and people, with regard to the Talmud and its relation to the original traditional law, is thus succinctly stated by Chiarini: "According to them, the authors and compilers of the Talmud, instead of giving us the fruits of their meditations and labors, have only transmitted to us in writing the things which they knew by heart, having heard them from their preceptors or from their ancestors, and these latter, in their turn from their preceptors or their ancestors, up to the Seventy Ancients and to Aaron, and to Moses himself." [1]

58. The law received by Moses from the Almighty, on Sinai, was doctrinal as well as governmental. We see this in the portions that have been placed in writing, and it must have been the same with the oral. So far as this law was governmental it might be considered that the multitude whose daily conduct was to be regulated thereby, should be made and kept more familiar with it; hence it is found in large part put in writing distinctly and rendered thus more accessible to all. As to the doctrinal portion, however, the populace, under the Old Dispensation and before the birth of the Redeemer, needed not to be so fully informed regarding at least the

[1] Chiarini, *Le Talmud*, Vol. I, p. 5.

deeper mysteries of faith as did and do those who came after the delivery and preaching of the Gospel. The advent of the Savior of the World, His crucifixion and death, operated an essential change in this regard and rendered it necessary that all men, called to be His disciples, should be personally apprised of the Trinity, of the Divinity of Christ, of the Fall of Man and of the Atonement.

59.   The Old Dispensation was, as it were, the prophetic stage of true religion, the promise and indication of what was to come in the day of the Messiah and through and with Him, and a preparation for it.   If, as is contended, the great religious truths, to which we have last referred, were communicated by God to Moses upon Sinai, they called for careful keeping during the succeeding time to the appearance of the expected Messiah: and this despite the fact that it was unnecessary, perhaps inadvisable, that, under the old order, these sacred mysteries be proclaimed to the masses.   It is reasonable, therefore, to conclude that the oral law of the ancient Jews was of two kinds, esoteric and exoteric; in other words, reserved and open.   Walton, in his Prolegomena, p. 53, affirms that such was the case.   "The first kind of Cabal," he says, "is of those who lived before Christ.   It contained indeed the mystic and secret exposition of Scripture, not written but delivered by word of mouth, and this not by all but by the elder and wiser ones."

60.   "This," says Drach, dealing with the same original and purer Cabala, "was the occult part of the theological science.   It treated of the nature of

God and His attributes, of spirits and of the visible world. In its varied teaching it grounded itself upon certain theoretic traditions, and on the interpretation, which is called symbolic, mystical, anagogic of the text of the Old Testament. This interpretation was also traditional as we shall see later. It was, if we choose so to style it, the divine philosophy, or the speculative theology of the Synagogue; its sacred physics and sacred metaphysics: in a word its treatises *de Deo et Ejus Attributis* and *De Deo Creatore* in all their extent. We may add that, neither were the essentials of the treatises *De SS. Trinitate* and *De Incarnatione* forgotten." [1]

61. It is not meant to here concede that there is nothing in the Old Testament, which was the written divine law of the Old Dispensation, indicative of the belief by the Ancient Hebrews in the Trinity and in the Divinity of the Messiah who then was to come. On the contrary, it is a conviction shared by many students that in numerous passages of the early Sacred Writings, these holy dogmas are unmistakably referred to. Our own sole purpose, in this present chapter, is to demonstrate that, even if, for the sake of discussion, we yield this point, no conclusion can be fairly drawn therefrom, to the effect that the great religious truths we are considering were utterly unknown to Moses and his people.

62. We might, indeed, go further in this same line and grant without fatal injury to our cause, that both the written and the oral law of the Olden

---

[1] *L'Harmonie entre l'Eglise et la Synagogue,* par le Chevalier P. B. L. Drach, Vol. I, preface, p. xi.

Jews were without traces of these two great dogmas.
We can know by our natural reason something about
God. His Existence, His Omnipotence, His Infinite
Wisdom, His creation of the Universe and His Providence, etc., are made known by His works. But the
Divine Being and Nature constitute a boundless
ocean, upon which the unaided human understanding
can have but a narrow horizon. Revelation, however,
has come to the assistance of natural reason and extended our knowledge of God. But no one can prove
that it was absolutely necessary that all revelation
should be given to mankind at one time: or that, if
so given, it must have been from the beginning fully
developed or entirely understood.

63. Even, therefore, were it proven (the very
reverse of which is the case) that Our Lord Jesus
Christ was absolutely the first one to proclaim to
men the great dogmas of the Trinity and of His own
Godhood, or to make clear to them what had before
Him been only vaguely intimated, this fact would
have furnished in itself no valid objection to Christian faith. In order to discredit in this way the
New Dispensation, it would be necessary to demonstrate that the Sacred Writings of the Old Law positively conflict with the Gospel teaching in these regards. In other words, the objection we are now
considering would be sufficiently met by showing
that there is nothing in the Old Testament which con-
travenes in any way these holy doctrines, which
some erroneously believe were first introduced into
the world by the Christian Church.

CHAPTER II.

"In the Head of the Book."

64.   It is a propositon which has been much discussed: "Are the dogmas of the Holy Trinity and of the Divinity of Christ indicated, with any clearness, in the Old Testament?"   For Christians this is not a controlling question, inasmuch as even a necessary negative answer to it would not be subversive of our accepted beliefs in these respects.   It can be proven that the olden Hebrews had an oral law as well as a written one, the former of which was supplementary and interpretative.   Furthermore, the Lord might well have reserved the fuller exposition of these profounder religious truths for the time of the coming of Christ.

65.   It must, however, be a strong argument in support of the Christian teaching upon these two sacred subjects, to be able to show affirmatively, from Holy Scripture itself, that the ancient Jews were cognizant of these divine mysteries and accepted them as true.

66.   It should not be held essential to the making out of a case in this regard that a multitude of texts be marshalled.   If only it be clear and to the point, one single citation from Holy Writ should be accepted as sufficient, for this purpose.   Or, if no one particular verse is to be found, which of itself unmistakably states these great mysteries, the result

should be the same, if several sentences or paragraphs be shown, all fairly admitting of such a construction.

67.   In the latter event, of course, the greater the number of these suggestive passages, which can be thus made use of, the stronger the case is established. A criticism, or doubt, which might tend to neutralize, for our present purposes, one such reference if unsupported, must lose force if leveled against an accumulation of passages, all of similar import.

68.   In Psalms 39:8, 9 (40:7), we find a verse which is repeated in Hebrews 10:7, and which in the Douay translation reads as follows: "In the head of the book it is written of me that I should do thy will." It is not necessary to here argue over the respective merits of the different renditions of these texts, or to discuss their true meaning and application, for the reason that we do not rely upon them as links in our chain of evidence. It is a fact, however, worthy of note in this connection, that it is in the very opening chapter of Genesis, the actual "head of the book," that we find what many consider the first scriptural showing of the Trinity.

69.   The opening words of the Old Testament are translated ordinarily as follows: "In the beginning God created heaven and earth. And the earth was void and empty, and darkness was upon the face of the deep; and the Spirit of God moved over the waters."

70.   Now the first three words of this passage may be rendered "by the Beginning," etc., or "through the Beginning," and the first verse be made

thereby to read: "By (or through) the Beginning, God created heaven and earth," etc. "Beginning" in such a case would have its legitimate meaning of Principle, in the sense of First Cause or Origin; and it would be applicable, in this passage of Holy Scripture and others of kindred signification, to the Son of God, upon the theory that to the Second Person of the Adorable Trinity is to be assigned in some particular way the origin of finite things, or upon the theory that it was intended to be indicated, in the first and second verses of Genesis, that the Son and the Holy Ghost, with the Father, were acting in the great work of creation.

71. The New Testament is a recognized key to the old. Even though some refuse to acknowledge the inspiration of the Gospels, practically all concede their utility, in the work of explaining and interpreting the more ancient portions of the Scriptures. We may, therefore, legitimately turn to the Holy Evangelists for light in this particular regard. Saint John opens his Gospel with the following words: "In the beginning was the Word, and the Word was with God, and the Word was God. The same was in the beginning with God. All things were made by Him; and without Him was made nothing that was made." While it is true that the passage last quoted may be construed so as to only declare in a general way that God, the Son, equally with God the Father and God the Holy Ghost, performed the work of creation, on the other hand it appears that we have here another inspired expression which may be read as harmonizing with the interpretation suggested for

Genesis, to the effect that the Word of God, there named the Beginning or Principle, was in some particular way connected with the original creation; and this, of course, without suggesting the exclusion of the Father and the Holy Ghost from the same divine work.

72.   Saint Paul, Coll. 1:18, calls Christ "The Beginning," and this immediately after having written as follows: "For in him were all things created in heaven and on earth, visible and invisible, whether thrones or dominations, or principalities or powers: all things were created by him and in him. And he is before All: and by him all things consist." Coll. 1:16, 17.

73.   In the Apocalypse (Revelation of St. John) 1:8, are these impressive words: "I am Alpha and Omega, the beginning and the end, saith the Lord God, who is, who was and who is to come, the Almighty." That it is Christ who is here particularly spoken of is clear, because the book itself opens with the announcement that it is "the Revelation of Jesus Christ," [1] and, in the preceding verses, the Sacred Writer deals with Christ, reciting what He had done for the Children of the Church. Furthermore, the passage immediately antecedent tells us of Him who is to come in the clouds, so that "every eye shall see him *and they that pierced him.*" Saint John again uses the same expression in Chap. 21, verse 6, of the same inspired book, "I am Alpha and Omega, the be-

[1] Likewise, near the close, Chap. 22, verse 16, it is said: "I Jesus have sent to you my angel to testify to you these things in the Churches. I am the root and stock of David, the bright and morning star."

ginning and the end," and repeats it in Chap. 22, verse 13.[1]

74. Even in our own English, we are not precluded from giving to the particular terms employed in the translation of the opening words of Genesis, which is in ordinary use among us, the construction above suggested. The preposition "in" has many meanings and is used to express a greater variety of relations than any other. The dictionaries define it under seventeen different heads, and show it to be a proper synonym for several particles of its class. Of these definitions one reads thus: "of means or instruments: By means; with; by; through." Among other examples of this particular use of our word, the same lexicon quotes the following, from Gal. 3:8: "In thee shall all nations be blessed." Another definition is as follows: "of cause or occasion; from; because of; on account of; for the sake of." It, therefore, seems clear that, even in our own language, we may take these words "in the beginning" as having the same sense as they would have had if "by the

---

[1] In connection with the idea that the Son of God is mentioned in the very opening of the Old Testament, we may call attention to the fact that the New Testament also begins with a reference to Christ: "The book of the generation of Jesus Christ, the Son of David, the Son of Abraham." Matt. 1:1. The New Testament, and for that matter the entire Holy Scripture, ends also, practically, with the Savior's name. The last words of the Apocalypse, or Revelation of Saint John, are as follows: "He that giveth testimony of these things saith: surely I come quickly: Amen. Come Lord Jesus. The Grace of Our Lord Jesus Christ be with you all." Verses 20, 21. It will be observed that the Apocalypse really ends with verse 20, and with the words "Come Lord Jesus." The twenty-first and last verse is merely the Apostle's own postscript, conveying to his readers his own blessing.

Beginning," "with the Beginning," or "through the Beginning," had been employed.

75. But it may be urged, that, after all, we are not mainly concerned with the shape in which English translators have presented to us the first sentence of Genesis; that we are more interested to know the true meaning of the text as it is in the original.

76. The word in Hebrew, rendered in our current English translations by "in the beginning" is *"bereschit."* The Rabbinical writers were well aware that, in the construction appearing here, this word *"Bereschit"* could be regarded as in itself suggestive of the idea of a divine Personage; for it is said in the Talmud (Meghilla, fol. 8 recto), that the seventy-two Ancients, who gave to the world the Septuagint, changed in their Greek version, the order of the words as appearing in the original, and placed "in the beginning" after instead of before "God created"; and this that King Ptolemy, at whose instance the Septuagint was produced, might not conclude that the Jews worshipped two Gods instead of one, and that the second was created by or proceded from the other.[1] In the Thosephot or Additions to the Gloss of Rabbi Salomon Yarhhi, known commonly as Rasschi, found on the margins of copies of the Talmud, it is said: "The Greeks know that the name of God should always be assigned the first place. Ptolemy might have thought that there were

[1] Chevalier P. B. L. Drach, *De l'Harmonie entre l'Eglise et la Synagogue*, Vol. I, pp. 287, 288. Paul Isaac Hershon, *Genesis, with a Talmudic Commentary*, translated by Rev. M. Wolkenberg (Sam'l Bagster & Sons, London), p. 5.

two divinities, and that *Bereschit* signified a Creator as well as *Elohim*, the third word of the same verse." And Rabbi Salomon Yarhhi himself in his gloss to the Talmudical text above quoted, thus explains: "to the end that the King should not consider that *bereschit* was the name of a divinity, that there are two divinities and that the second proceeds from the first."

77. The motive assigned by the Rabbinical Writers for the change thus made by the Seventy-two Ancients in the succession of the opening words of Genesis, as these words were set down in their translation, is not satisfactory; for the Greek, unlike the Hebrew, has case endings, and "God," as appearing at this place in the Septuagint, is in the nominative form and could not, therefore, have suggested to any one the idea that it was intended to be an object of the verb "created." So the verb itself appears in both versions in the singular and, therefore, it could not be held as suggestive here of a plurality of Gods. But it is fair to presume that there was some motive which impelled the Septuagints to make the change in question, and it is probable that the motive was to avoid the possibility of the Pagan Greeks finding in this passage any intimation of the mystery of the Trinity, which presents not a plurality of Gods but a plurality of persons in a One and Only God. Saint Jerome, who was thoroughly versed in the Hebrew, dealing with this subject, while accepting as one reason for the change we are now discussing, the fear that, without the alteration, King Ptolemy might consider that

here was evidence that the Jews worshipped two
Gods, adds: "Finally, wheresoever in Scripture any
sacred reference is made to the Father, and the Son
and the Holy Ghost, either they have explained it
differently, or they have been entirely silent: so that
they might satisfy the King and not divulge the mystery of the faith." [1]

78.   Some further attention should be given to
the foregoing quotation from the Thosephot: "The
Greeks knew that the name of God should always be
assigned the first place.   Ptolemy might have
thought that there were two divinities, and that
Bereschit signified a creator as well as *Elohim*, the
third word of the same verse."   Knowing the profound veneration in which the older Jews held the
Almighty and, also, His Sacred Name, and the careful efforts which they made to show on all occasions
and in every way their reverence, we may accept as
true the statement made, as shown above, that the
Divine Name was given the right of precedence,
where grammar and sense permitted.   We should,
therefore, be slow to believe that a rule, founded
upon so high a motive, was needlessly violated in this
instance and that, in a sentence of such importance
as the one we have now under consideration, the
place of honor should be withheld from the divine
Name and accorded to a mere adverb of time, of no
consequence in itself, and which, from such a point
of view, might have been dispensed with entirely.

79.   The importance of this particular sentence
arises not only from the circumstance that therein

[1] Prologus in Genesin, ad Desiderium. T. IX, p. 3.

one of the most momentous facts in the history of
God's relation toward the entire universe is announced, but to the other circumstance, also, that it
is the opening sentence of the entire Sacred Scripture, the very "head of the Book." The interpretation, consequently, which Modern Jews and some
others would put upon the passage, if correct, would
bring it about that all of the Written Revelation
that we have, which might so much better have begun
with the Name of Him who is Lord of All, opens in
fact with a word of minor importance; a word equivalent to our English adverb, originally.[1]

80. Another thought in this same line is worthy
of mention. If it be true that *bereschit*, as here used
in the original Hebrew and given the place of highest
honor in the Old Testament, carries with it no other
meaning than the one which would be suggested in
similar connection by our English adverb *originally*,
or by the phrase "in the beginning" employed ad-
verbially, what at all, may we ask, can be the particular significance or utility of this word as thus introduced into this sentence? Shall we interpret it
as expressive of the idea that heaven and earth have

---

[1] Against this particular argument the fact may be urged
that the verb in this sentence (created) precedes the name
Elohim (God), and it may be reasoned therefrom that this
arrangement contradicts the testimony above quoted, to the
effect that the ancient Jews gave always the first place to the
name of God. The position of honor in the sentence under
consideration, and the position of honor at the same time in
the entire Scriptures, must be its very head or opening; and,
if *Bereschit* be conceded as being one form of the divine Name,
the subsequent placing of *Elohim* would not detract from the
reverence already shown to the Almighty, by putting His
sacred name in one of its forms, "at the head of the book."

been created from eternity, and that all in this connection which has been done in time was the moving
of the Spirit of God over the waters, with the re-
sultant reduction of the original chaos to order and
system?   Certainly not, for what motive can we
imagine as having influenced the Almighty to make
from eternity a "void and empty" earth, to bring
into being before all time a mere chaos, while post-
poning, during a period immeasurably long, the
work of developing and perfecting the first rude
creation?

81.   Shall it be maintained, on the other hand,
that the *bereschit* here used was intended to announce
merely that the making of heaven and earth was the
first act of divine creation, and that, before this,
nothing had been that was finite?   Against this latter
interpretation is the fact that the opening sentences
of Genesis reveal to us only God and heaven and
earth, and describe God as precedent and heaven and
earth as coming into being at His command.   And if
it be that making heaven and earth were the very
first creative acts of God, this fact, in the absence
of all contrary suggestion, finds sufficient expression
without the word *bereschit;* whereas if, as a matter
of fact, other finite things had been made by God before the heaven and earth, then the term in question,
if used in the sense last presented, would be untrue.

82.   Moreover, the words "in the beginning" cannot convey this last considered meaning, with any
distinctness; for, while they may suggest the broader
idea that nothing finite existed before our heaven
and earth, equally may they be held as setting forth

no more than that what Genesis records as the actual beginning for our Universe only, leaving open the question as to whether there were not other Universes created in addition to our own and older that it and beyond the limit of our present knowledge. Other forms will suggest themselves to the intelligent mind more precise and clear than this one, for the purpose of expressing the thought that our heaven and earth had absolutely no predecessors of any description in the order of created things.

83. The Talmud may not present absolutely indisputable support for the position assumed above, but it must be remembered that this work is that of Jewish Rabbis, who lived after the time of our Blessed Redeemer upon earth, and after the great controversy between Christianity and Modern Judaism had arisen, and a bitter animosity had sprung up among the Jews against Christ and His sacred teaching. What, therefore, the Rabbinical Writers wrote in this connection, they wrote ordinarily with caution, through fear that what was put down might come to the knowledge of the Christian and be used against themselves in the great controversy they were ever carrying on against Christianity. But enough has escaped these writers and commentators from time to time, to justify the conclusion that secretly they regarded as divine the Messiah, whom they continued so long and vainly to expect, and to warrant the conclusion that, had such a Messiah as they hoped to see appeared among them, he would have been proclaimed the Son of the Most High.

84. The Messiah is often referred to in Holy

Scripture and by the Rabbins as the Just, or
Righteous One; [1] and in the Talmud, in the treatise
entitled Yoma, folio 38, the work of Creation is at-
tributed to the virtue or force of the Just One. The
Zohar,[2] which, whatever might be its origin, is a work

[1] For instance, Jeremias 33:14, 15, 16; 23:5, 6; Acts 3:14;
7:52; 22:14.

[2] The Zohar purports to be a work by Simon Yochi, who
lived during the end of the first and beginning of the second
century after Christ, and it is supposed to set forth in writing
the revelation which God had given to Adam in Paradise, carried down the ages through the mouths of Patriarchs and
Prophets, until reduced at last to writing as above stated.
Many assert, for reasons which are summarized by Rev. C. D.
Ginsburg, LL. D., in the *Encyclopædia Britannica,* Vo. Kabbalah, that the true author was one Moses de Leon, A. D. 1300
to 1306. Others hold the view expressed by S. M. Schiller
Szinezi, M. A., University Library, Cambridge, in the same
Encyclopædia, Vo. Midrash, to the effect that "the nucleus of
the book is of Mischinic times and R. Shimeon Yohai was the
author of the Zohar in the same sense that R. Yohanan was
the author of the Palestinian Talmud; *i. e.,* he gave the first
impulse to the composition of the book. But R. Mosheh de
Leon, on the other hand, was the first not only to copy and
disseminate the Zohar in Europe, but, also, to disfigure it by
sundry explanatory interpolations." See, also, his note 7.
Be the true relation of Moses de Leon to this work what it
may, the fact remains that the Rabbins of De Leon's time,
practically as a body, conceded at once its authenticity and
verity; and it is competent for that reason if for no other to
serve, wherever it can be so employed, as corroboration of the
Christian contention, that the cardinal dogmas held by the
Church of Christ were known to the Jews under the old dispensation and were taught with more or less reserve, even in
the Modern Synagogue, while the latter was awaiting the Messiah it was vainly expecting.
The fact that the Zohar contains, besides many unmistakable
references to the Trinity, the Messiah's Divinity, etc., extravagant recitals of various sorts and sundry theories, which are
borrowed from various forms of paganism, takes, of course,
from its probative force in this present connection, but is far
from destroying it. Similar charges may be justly advanced
against the Talmud and other Rabbinical productions. Such
aberrations, however, go only to show the lengths of absurdity

written by Jews and for Jews, contains several passages which are exactly in line with the arguments that have been above presented. In fol. 1, col. 10, it is said: "*Bereschit* answers to the mystery included in the name Jehova." In fol. 8, col. 30, is the following: "with regard to these words of the text: *In the Beginning God Created*, etc., Rabbi Hhiya explains in this way: It is written, the *fear of God is the Beginning of Wisdom*. Should the Sacred Author have said: *the fear of* God is the end of Wisdom, and not the commencement, since Wisdom is the degree which leads to the fear of God? But he desired to speak of the Heavenly and Eternal Wisdom. He wished to tell us that the fear of God is the first door at which we enter in order to approach the Eternal Wisdom. The prefix *beth* before the word *reschit*, Beginning, proclaims that there are in the Beginning Two who are united in One, two points united, whereof one is hidden and invisible, and the other shows to be discovered. And because they are inseparable, the word *reschit* is in the singular: one, not two. Who receives one receives equally the other, all being but one. For he is himself his name, and his name is one, as it is written: "And let them know that thou alone hast the name Jehova." Psalm 82 (83):19.

85. The extract just given is a plain statement from a Jewish source unquestionably, that the

to which the Synagogue went, after the Almighty had withdrawn from it His divine guardianship, without justifying the assumption that none of its teachings were truly ancestral or taking from the force as admissions of statements made from time to time, probably through inadvertence, favorable to Christianity.

Bereschit, which is the opening word of the Holy Scripture is intended to name a Person, and not merely to express time when or an order of succession; that the Person so named is identical with Jehova; that this Person, *Bereschit* is of dual nature, one thereof divine that is hidden and invisible, the other human and hence visible, and both natures are joined together inseparably and made one.

86.   Again in the same work, fol. 15, col. 58: "In the Beginning, mystery of the wisdom.   In the Beginning, this is the Word, who corresponds to the degree of Wisdom, and he is called *Reschit.*"

Fol. 20, col. 79: "*Beth, Reschit,* this is the Wisdom, as Jonathan [1] construes *by the wisdom,* because this *Reschit* is the *second in the number.*   And he is called *Reschit,* Beginning (or Principle) because the *Celestial Crown, always invisible,* not making yet a number,[2] the *Reschit* is the *second;* this is why it is said: God produced (begot) *bethreschit* (the second Principle).   Furthermore, since the Wisdom of above or on high is the Principle, similarly the Wisdom of below [3] is also the Principle.   For this reason the letter *beth,* two, must not be separated from the name *Reschit.*   We call this *Bereschit,* the Word and such it is."

[1] Jonathan-ben-Huziel, reputed compiler of the *Jerusalem Targum on the Pentateuch,* etc.

[2] "The Celestial Crown, always invisible not making yet a number," refers to God the Father, "always invisible" because never incarnated.   "Not yet making number" is a form of expression meaning first.

[3] By "Wisdom of above" (or on high) is meant the Messiah's divinity, and by "Wisdom of below" His humanity.

87. In the Zohar, also, fol. 19, col. 76: "In the Beginning, *Reschit*, God created. Mystery included in this verse: You shall give to Jehova the *Reschit* (first fruits) of your dough in consecrated cakes (Num. 15:19, 20, 21). This is the Celestial Wisdom; it is it which is the *Reschit*.[1]

88. The word "God," as we find it in our English versions, in the first chapter of Genesis, "In the beginning God created," etc., is in the original Hebrew *Elohim*, which is in plural form, used however, in a singular sense, inasmuch as its verb is in the singular. This arrangement or mode of construction is found repeatedly in the Old Testament and has occasioned much discussion, which is not possible to consider at any length in this present article. Suffice it to say that we should suppose that this method of expression, employed in the Older Scripture, is not without its special significance; and we may well consider that there is here a striking commingling as it were of the grammatical numbers in these particular verbal expressions, in order to intimate that there is in the subject spoken of, God, a mysterious combination of unity with plurality, such as is taught in the dogma of the Holy Trinity, one God and three Divine Persons.

89. The second paragraph of Genesis reads: "And the Earth was void and empty, and darkness was upon the face of the deep; and the Spirit of God moved over the waters." This language seems clearly to indicate an action successive to the one related in

[1] See P. B. L. Drach: *De l'Harmonie entre l'Eglise et la Synagogue,* Vol. I, p. 286.

the first sentence, or rather to describe a second
stage of the same general action. First, we are told
that "in the Beginning God created heaven and
earth," that is the entire universe. But, so far at
least as the earth was concerned, its primal condition was one of chaos, "void and empty." Subsequently, "the Spirit of God moved over the waters,"
etc. It is to be strongly presumed that an author
uses every one of his words advisedly; and for this
reason, in the interpretation of what he has written,
every word must be given, if possible, some office and
meaning. Why, in this case, tell us that "the
Spirit of God moved over the waters," if no particular thought or idea was to be conveyed by
the use of the term "Spirit," or if the meaning
was to be no more than would have been conveyed
had it been written simply "God moved over the
waters?"

90. The purpose of this paragraph cannot be, as
some maintain, to merely mention the rushing of a
mighty wind over or across the chaos, for, even had
such an incident occurred at that incipient stage of
the great work of creation, it would be scarcely
worthy of special recording in the impressive and
highly condensed account of the origin of the universe set forth in the first chapter of Genesis. And
such a rushing of the wind would be scarcely mentioned as a bare fact, without detailing at the same
time the particular purpose for which it was sent and
the end which it accomplished.

91. Furthermore, the first sentences of the Holy
Writ show to us God Himself as the Great Worker.

He is the subject of the active verbs, the direct and immediate Actor throughout. In the text under examination the "Spirit of God" is presented in this same positive fashion, as acting, primarily, directly and of itself, and not permissively or responsively only. This paragraph telling us that "the Spirit of God moved over the waters" is preceded immediately by the one declaring that God created heaven and earth and followed also immediately by the one reciting the divine creation of light. If, therefore, it be that which we translate here by the words "Spirit of God," means only a great wind, we find a passage relative to a mere created thing, sandwiched in as it were, between two passages that deal solely with acts of the Almighty Maker of the Universe.

92. The Hebrew word translated in our English versions by "moved" is considered by many as having here the meaning of hovering or fluttering over, as it clearly has in Deut. 32:11, where the eagle is spoken of as hovering or fluttering over her young. In the Babylonian Talmud, Treatise *Hhagiga*, fol. 15, recto, giving the saying of Ben Zoma, this meaning is accepted, as also the fact that the particular action under consideration was one of the Holy Spirit; "And the Spirit of God hovered over the face of the water, as a dove which hovers over its young and does not touch them." The Talmud of Jerusalem, also purporting to cite Ben Zoma in this same connection, is to the following effect: "There is here *hovering*, and it is said elsewhere (Deut. 32:11) as the eagle guards over her nest, hovers over her eaglets; since the hovering which is used elsewhere

signifies to touch and not to touch, the hovering here signifies, also, to touch and not to touch." [1]

93.   Still others here assign to this same Hebrew verb, translated for us, in Gen. 1:2, "moved," the sense of brooding, as where the bird broods on her nest and thus causes the germs within the eggs to develop and come forth eventually as little birds.[2]

94.   From all these reasons, it seems manifest that the verb "moved," as we find it here used in our English versions, should not be given the narrow meaning of mere motion on the part of an active agent, as where the wind blows across the surface of the land or ocean. It is entitled to carry in the passage now in question, that deeper and nobler sense which also belongs to it as expressive of a quickening or stirring into life or activity of an object which had been inert, just as the genial breath of spring wakes mother earth from her winter sleep and moves her to put forth again her leaves and blossoms.

95.   Other passages might be cited from Holy Scripture, going to confirm the truth, which it is thought is also shown in the words from Gen. 1:2, now under consideration; which truth is that the Holy Ghost is one of the Divine Persons, Who constitute and are the One God, and who were, as such, Participators in the work of Creation. Suffice it now to refer merely to Psa. 32 (33):6; 103 (104):30; Job 33:4.

96.   We may conclude this study by calling at-

[1] Drach, *De l'Harmonie entre l'Eglise et la Synagogue,* Vol. I, pp. 303, 464.

[2] See Hasting's *Dictionary of the Bible,* Vol. II, p. 403.

tention to the fact that the probability that the
opening lines of Sacred Scripture contain a manifestation of the glorious dogma of the Holy Trinity is
greatly increased by the circumstance that two passages are to be found here, distinct though in close
conjunction, both of them fairly open to constructions supporting the particular view herein advocated, together with the similarly suggestive use of a
divine name in the plural form with a singular verb.
When a second and then a third reputable witness
follow a first, testifying all in the same way, with regard to some particular fact, when one pregnant circumstance is joined to another, and then a third is
added, all pointing to the same general conclusion;
there is in either case an increase of probative force,
which is not two or threefold merely, but manifold.

CHAPTER III.

Elohim.

97. We have touched, briefly, in a preceding paper, upon the repeated use, in the Old Testament, of the plural, *Elohim,* as one of the Divine Names, accompanied by a verb in the singular. Gen. 1:1, was particularly referred to in this connection: "In the beginning God (*Elohim*) created [1] heaven and earth." The verbal arrangement shown here is odd and very striking, and it merits careful study, particularly with a view to ascertaining what bearing it may have, if any, upon the dogma of the Holy Trinity.

98. This seeming disagreement, as to number, between the subject and its verb, in Gen. 1:1, and elsewhere in Holy Scripture, is remarkable for more reasons than one. As the opening sentences of the Bible deal solely with the Creator and His works, in them, least of all, should we expect to find carelessness in composition. Hence we should hold, if possible, that there is in fact no error, or inadvertence here, and seek for some reason which shall in some other way satisfactorily explain the apparent incongruity.

[1] In the Hebrew, "created" has, even in the tense here used, a singular and a plural form, varying in this respect so as to be in agreement with its subject. For this reason, the remarkable construction we are now considering, the giving of a plural subject to a singular verb in this tense, is apparent in the original, though not shown in our English translations.

52

99. Without discussing now the question of inspiration, it will at least be admitted that those who gave to us the several books of the Old Testament, knew enough of their own grammar to be aware that subject and verb should agree in number. The seeming anomaly, which we are considering, even if it escaped the attention of the author, must have attracted the notice of every intelligent reader, from the earliest times; and, unless there was then some general original understanding as to its true signification, the result must have been constant criticism and discussion.[1]

100. If further proof be needed to show that the use of this odd construction, to be found in Gen. 1:1, was deliberate and with a purpose, we have it in the fact that in one shape or another, it finds several repetitions in the Old Testament. Had it appeared in Scripture but once, we might charge the occurrence to lack of care, but this cannot well be done, considering the frequent repetition of this form.

101. The theory has been put forward to the effect that the giving of a plural name to God, in these Scriptural passages, indicates that the Older Hebrews were first polytheists and then monotheists. Were this theory correct, it would imply that the retention of a manifestly pagan designation of the Deity was throughout the result of error and negli-

---

[1] We shall later show that the early Christians, of Hebrew lineage, attacked successfully their unconverted Brethren upon this very ground, that the Scriptural use of the plural "Elohim" with a singular verb, was a disclosure of the Trinity. There is no evidence to support the proposition that this thought was new with the first Christians.

gence on the part of the compilers, that those who afterward received and used the work disregarded these lapses, or carelessly overlooked them, and that all the copyists who reproduced it showed the same indifference in regard to them. The reasons just stated as going to show that the repeated use of these mixed constructions in the Older Scriptures must have been deliberate, apply here with increased force, to exclude the idea that the monotheists, who have given us the Old Testament in its present shape, would have chosen from the ancient text or texts another name for Jehova, that by nature was suggestive of idolatry, or that was calculated to perpetuate the memory of a former dominance of idolatrous worship throughout Israel.

102. With some exceptions, touched upon further on, and which cannot affect this argument, *Elohim,* when coupled in Holy Scripture with a singular verb, applies, like the name Jehova, to the one and only God. If, despite its own plurality of form, *Elohim* has this monotheistic sense, when controlled or explained by its verb in the singular, and if this was also the case in the time of the alleged compiler or compilers of the first books of the Old Testament, how shall it be proven that it had a different meaning in Israel, previous to the first appearance of the Pentateuch?

103. In searching for motive, we should not only study the character and importance of the act involved, but also place ourselves in the situation of the actor, so as to understand his thoughts, feelings and expectations. If we can do this here, we may

safely disregard many suggested solutions, which
must seem to us trivial in their nature, and, likewise,
to all such as are not in accordance with the probable ideas, mental habits and sentiments of the
authors of the Older Scriptures.

104. The reasons which convince us that the repeated use in Holy Writ of *Elohim*, with singular
verbs, was deliberate, should serve also to convince
us that the actuating motive in the case must have
been strong. It is true that Ancient Israel, from
the time at least of the appearance, in its present
shape, of the first book of the Old Testament, was
monotheistic; but the nations about her worshipped
many and varied gods, and her spiritual leaders were
engaged in a constant struggle to restrain her children from adoring the idols of their pagan neighbors.[1] Nevertheless, the writers or compilers of the
older Sacred Books of Scripture referred in many
places to the one God of their Fathers by a name
which literally means "gods," and which might,
therefore, have suggested to strangers the notion
that, after all, the Children of Abraham, Isaac and
Jacob were in fact and had always been polytheists,
and might have served as a pretense for the evil-
disposed at home to practice idolatry. At best, to
give to the Almighty Jehova a name, which equally
fits the false gods of paganism, is not upon its face
a act of reverence toward the One, Omnipotent and
Eternal God; and, when we find earnest and enlight-

[1] Even in our day it is argued by some, and from these same
passages, that the Older Jews were originally polytheists and
that the Elohim of the Holy Writ, in so far as it is applied to
the Almighty is a survival from an older polytheistic literature.

ened believers doing this, we must consider that they
were forced to it by some strong reason.

It is not possible, within the compass of a single
article, to discuss all of the explanatory theories
which have been suggested in this connection; but
some of the principal ones among those that are
opposed to the solution which we deem the correct
one may be shown, we think, to be without sufficient
weight or dignity to have influenced the writing into
our Sacred Books of the forms now in question.

105.   The contention that several names are given
to God in the Old Testament for the purpose of presenting Him to us in His different aspects (the office
of *Elohim* being to designate him as Creator and
Preserver of the Universe) might merit attention if
the question were merely *why* the Almighty was
variously named.   *Elohim* has its singular form, *El*
or *Eloah*, and the suggestion under consideration
does not of itself answer the true question which is
before us: Why should a name of any sort in its
plural form, with the accompanying verb in the
singular, be applied to the Almighty?

106.   We are told that *Elohim* in these passages
"designates the fullness of divine power, and is
rightly called by Delitzsch a plural of intensity." [1]
What is meant by the quotation last given must be
that when the term *Elohim* is applied to God, as acting or creating, it represents Him as exerting a degree or "intensity" of power different from, or
rather superior to that exercised in doings which are
credited to Him under the other names, by which He

[1] Schaff-Herzog, *Religious Encyclopædia,* Vol. I, p. 719.

is designated, such as Jehova, El Shaddai, etc. In its usual sense, and the one clearly intended for it here, "fullness" conveys the idea of measurement or limitation, and measurement or limitation has to do only with finite things. There can be no more "fullness" in connection with infinitude than there can be emptiness. Granting space to be infinite, what can be its "fullness," or its "intensity"? We speak of the "fullness of time," but not of the fullness of eternity.[1] The difficulty in creation is to make anything at all out of nothing; and the making of the universe out of nothing could require no greater "fullness" or "intensity" of action, on the part of Omnipotence, than the calling into being similarly of a grain of dust.

107. We are reminded by some that there is, in the Semitic tongues, such a thing as the Semitic Plural, consisting of the use of names plurally, for the purpose of expressing or suggesting vastness, immensity, mightiness, or superlative majesty, excellence, etc., in connection with particular persons or things. Such a rhetorical device might serve to exalt human beings, or finite things of any sort; but thoughtful minds should recognize the impossibility of honoring, by such means, the One and Only God,

---

[1] The word "fullness" is used sometimes in Holy Writ, in connection with God, as the synonym of "abundance" and without bringing in the thought whether that abundance be infinite or not. So it is employed occasionally to designate the totality of Divinity, if we may use such an expression; to signify, in other words, the aggregate of all of the Divine attributes, or the perfection of God's nature. Thus Saint Paul, writing of Jesus Christ, says, Coll. 2:9: "For in Him dwelleth the fullness of the God-head corporeally."

or of heightening in any way our conception of Him. It might flatter a great warrior, and raise him higher in the esteem of his associates, to declare that he is a host in himself; but could there be any true praise extended to the Infinite and Omnipotent Jehova, or could He be in any way uplifted, in the estimation of His creatures, by declaring Him to be equal to a million false deities? [1]   It is hard to believe that wise old monotheistic Jews would have risked the possibility of having the nation's belief upon this central point of its religion misapprehended at home and abroad simply that they might be enabled, by such means, to pay to the great Jehova an unbefitting compliment.

108.   The passage, Judges 16:23, is entitled to notice, where, in the original Hebrew, the false god Dagon is called *Elohim*, with a predicate verb following in the singular.   In this passage, we are told of the Philistines, rejoicing greatly over the capture of Samson and offering sacrifices, and *"saying:*

---

[1] We do find finite things used occasionally in Holy Scriptures to represent God, metaphorically; but this is not with a view to exalting the Almighty by such means, but for the purpose of reducing Him, as it were, to the level of our comprehension, so that we may more readily understand, or more fully appreciate, some divine attribute or characteristic, some divine action, or some particular relation or connection of the Omnipotent with His human creatures.   Men may be praised by speaking of them as in a class higher than that to which they really belong, or by proclaiming them as alone equal in any way, to several of their own class.   But, who is flattered by being compared to or with even a multitude of inferiors?   An oriental potentate may appreciate the use of the Semitic plural, in connection with himself, if the meaning be that his own greatness and eminence is equal to those combined of many Kings; but would he tolerate it, if the sense for him must be to liken him to a thousand slaves?

Our God hath delivered our enemy into our hands."
Be it observed, however, that we are here given the
words of the Philistines and not those of the Sacred
Writer: and the reasons suggested above against the
idea that the Semitic plural should be used by the
Ancient *Hebrew* Chroniclers, in connection with the
One Only and Omnipotent God, have no bearing,
when it comes to the idolatrous Philistines, speaking
of the false god Dagon, one only out of the innumerable fictitious deities of heathendom. Moreover, the
Philistines were close neighbors of the Jews, hence
not unapt to have borrowed from the latter, on this
occasion, a form of speech applied by the Chosen
People to the great Jehova.

109. Finally, on this subject, the name *Elohim*
was not, like the one *Jehova,* incommunicable: and
there was no reason for its not being used, even
among Hebrews, to designate the false divinities of
the Gentiles. In the same way, the name, God, is
applied, in our own time, to the One, true God,
whom alone we Christians adore, and say to Jupiter.
When the faithful Jews of old spoke of Chamos, or
Chemosh, Baal, Moloch, etc., as *Elohim,* they surely
had no intention to exalt those objects of false
heathen worship, by having recourse, in mentioning
them, to any pluralis excellentiæ, pluralis majestatis,
etc. On the contrary, they were more apt to have
considered the term *Elohim* as, in itself, suggestive
of that confusion which must have existed in pagan
minds of the time, between the false gods, abstractly
considered, whom their nations followed and the
numerous idols of wood, or clay, or stone, before

which the people, themselves, in various places, actually bowed down in worship and supplication.

110.   The Scriptural passages now under consideration have, as already intimated, furnished Christians, since the foundation of the Church, with an argument in support of the dogma of the Trinity.[1] It will scarcely be denied that the writers or compilers of the Old Testament were men of mental power, and it is fair to infer that they possessed at least ordinary prudence.   They must, therefore, have been aware of the fact that the peculiar grammatical constructions they used were subject to the interpretations that we know were assigned to them at least as early as the time of the first Christians.   Hence we are justified in claiming—despite the efforts of the modern Rabbis to obscure the fact—that the employment of such constructions confirms the contention that the Ancient Jews, as shown by Scripture, held to the doctrine of the Trinity.

[1] *"The Talmud of Jerusalem* (Berac., 34, a.) reports the disputes which arose between the Jews and the Christians of the first centuries of the Church on the mystery of the Trinity. The latter strove to prove it by the passages of the Bible, where the name of God is employed in the plural, and the first replied that the force of their reasoning was destroyed by the verb, which in those same passages was in the singular." Chiarini, *Le Talmud de Babylone,* Vol. I, p. 304, note 3.   The Christian argument here is confirmed and not destroyed by the suggestion of the verb's being in the singular.   The proposition is: can this strange intermingling of the two grammatical numbers while speaking of the Almighty, be explained from any standpoint other than our Christian one, that God is Triune?   It may be interesting to know that the Jews, who had become Christians, were victorious in these popular religious debates, as we may conclude from the fact that the Rabbis eventually forbade their people to engage in such controversies with Hebrew Christians.   *Genesis, with a Talmudic Commentary.*   Paul Isaac Hershon, pp. 22, 23, T. N.

111. While on this subject of the early discussions over this particular question, we may recall the fact that the disputants on these occasions were on both sides of Jewish blood, therefore Semites, familiar as such with the "Semitic plural," the "pluralis excellentiæ," etc., if any such expressions, in connection with the One Supreme God they worshipped, were in use in their own day, or in that of their ancestors. Furthermore, they must have been more familiar than we, of this distant generation, can be, with the customs, modes of thought and expression and as also with the traditions of their race. Hence if the use, in this particular connection, of a plural noun with a singular verb was a mere device of Hebrew rhetoric, and meant nothing more than to imply that the One God of Israel was equal to many or to all of the Gentile Gods combined, how is it that the early Rabbis seem to have been totally ignorant of a fact so important to them, and, to have made no use whatever of it in their theological battles with the early Christians? [1]

112. Numerous critics, by their contradictory reasonings and conflicting conclusions in this regard, have succeeded in convincing many that the use of *Elohim* in the Old Testament, so frequently and with different applications, constitutes one of the deepest puzzles of Exegetical Theology. The variations, however, in the meanings given in Holy Scripture to

[1] "These Rabbis and even Rashi, who flourished in the twelfth century, knew nothing of the modern pluralis excellentiæ, which is moreover inadmissible in personal appellations, etc." *Genesis, with a Talmudic Commentary,* by Paul Isaac Hershon, p. 22, translator's note, a.

this word should not be held as adding in any way to the mystery, if any there be; for scarcely a term of any importance is to be found in any civilized language that has not its several definitions. Even that most important and solemn of all words, God, has more meanings than one assigned to it in our dictionaries. A careful study of one of the uses to which this word *Elohim* is put in the Old Testament, other than as a name of the Deity, may enlighten rather than confuse us in this present enquiry. The name in question is found in Holy Writ applied to a Court, or rather, perhaps, to the judges who constituted the Court, taken collectively.[1] This word *Elohim* is not, however, used in the Old Testament as applicable to any and all courts, or to the magistrates composing the same; and the question arises, is there any particular kind of tribunal to which it was applied, and if so, what was the reason for the distinction?

[1] Exod. 21:5, 6: "And if the servant shall say: I love my master and my wife and children, I will not go free: his master shall bring him to the judges (in Hebrew Elohim)," etc.

Exod. 22:8, 9: "If the thief be not known, the master of the house shall be brought to the judges (Elohim) and he shall swear that he did not lay his hands upon his neighbor's goods," etc. See, also Psa. 81 (82), where "judges" should be read instead of "gods."

The Douay version has "gods" instead of "judges" in the two foregoing texts, the idea being that judges were here called "gods," because taking their authority from God. The King James Edition gives "judges" and the "Revised Edition" puts "God" in the text and "judges" in the margin.

These variations alter in no way the fact, as shown by the texts quoted and otherwise, that, among the ancient Hebrews, certain tribunals were named *Elohim.*

A careful consideration of Exod. 22:28, will convince us that the *Elohim* of the original stands also for "judges" and not for God or gods. See "Revised Edition," margin.

113. As in other countries with well organized governments there were, in Ancient Judea, courts great and small, high and low. A careful examination of the passages from Exod. 21:5, 6 and 22:8, 9, plainly show that the tribunals therein referred to were of inferior jurisdiction. Now history tells us that certain minor courts of the nation were composed of three judges; and to this day a somewhat similar tribunal exercises a certain authority among Orthodox Jews.[1]

114. The Talmud, Beracoth fo. 6. A, dealing with the presence of the Chekina among assemblages of men, says, among other things: "And whence do we know that the Chekina is also *with three* who are *sitting in judgment* (to judge). From the fact that it is said (Psa. 82 (81):1), he judges in the midst of judges (*Elohim*)." [2] And that *Elohim*, of the original Hebrew text, thus interpreted as meaning judges, referred to the Beth-Din, or tribunal of three, is proven not only by the very words themselves of the Talmud as last quoted, but also by the explicit gloss of the celebrated Raschi,[3] which is as

[1] "In large communities, however, there is a bet-din, consisting of at least three members, which sits daily, except on the Sabbath and holidays, and decides ritual as well as legal questions." *Jewish Encyclopedia,* Vo. Bet-Din. See, also, Drach, *De l'Harmonie entre l'Eglise et la Synagogue,* Vol. I, p. 437, and note 41.

[2] The sentence quoted above is omitted in some translations purporting to come from Beracoth, fo, 6, a, and to be found in certain selections of Talmudic extracts in English; but the words as given above may be found in Chiarini's *Translation of the Babylonian Talmud,* Vol. I, pp. 290, 291. Also in Hershon's *Genesis, with a Talmudic Commentary,* p. 18, verse 16.

[3] "Raschi, that is Rabbenu Shemoloh Yishaki (Solomon, Son of Isaac), whence by Christian writers he is called Isaacides

follows: "A beth-din is called *Elohim,* only when it is composed of three judges." [1]

115.   In the translations of the Babylonian Talmud by Michael L. Rodinski, Vol. VII (XV), Sanhedrin, Chap. 1, p. 5, we find the following: "And in the same way are to be interpreted the just cited verses 6 and 7 (Exodus 21), that the plaintiff has to bring his case before three only.   Therefore it may be said that the reason of Rabbi's decision is that because in the first verse it is written, 'the judges may condemn,' as in the last, three is meant, so it is with the word *Elohim,* mentioned before, which means judges," etc.

116.   The *Bereschit-Rabba,* dealing with the verse Gen. 19:24, "And the Lord (Jehova) rained upon Sodom and Gomorrha, brimstone and fire, from the Lord out of Heaven," reports the following teaching of the Rabbis: "R. Elieser teaches, throughout where there is in the text 'and Jehova,' we must understand God, with His tribunal.   For says R. Sal. Yarhhi, commenting on the verse from Exod. 12:29: 'And Jehova slew,' etc., the conjunction 'and' announces more than one person; as when it is said such a one and such a one."

117.   Chevalier P. B. L. Drach,[2] after quoting the above passages from the *Bereschit-Rabba,* and

(1040-1105) was the greatest Rabbi of the Middle Ages," etc. Dr. Schiller-Szinessy, M. A., Ph. D., Reader in Talmudic Literature, University of Cambridge, in *British Encyclopædia,* Vo. Raschi.

[1] Chiarini, *Le Talmud,* etc., Vol. I, p. 291, note 20.

[2] *De l'Harmonie entre l'Eglise et la Synagogue,* Vol. I, p. 436.

Yarhhi, continues as follows: "But, what is this tribunal which, with Jehova, punishes the guilty cities, which, with Jehova, strikes with death the first born of the Egyptians, determined to hold the Israelites enslaved, despite the reiterated commands of God? Every Rabbi will answer that Tribunal (in the Hebrew) means three persons, because, in the Mosaic law, the ordinary tribunal is composed of *three members*. Thus it is that the Talmud, Treatise *Rosch-Hosschana*, fol. 25, recto. says that 'every time three persons are brought together in a tribunal over Israel, they have the same authority as the tribunal of Moses.' "

118. If the above facts be true, and they seem supported by sufficient proofs, they militate strongly against the theory that, in the employment of *Elohim*, a plural form for the name of God, with a singular verb, we have simply the use of the Semitic plural; and they go to show that the lesser tribunals of Ancient Israel, composed of three, were dignified with this name *Elohim*, one of the appellations of the great Jehova, for the sole reason that they resembled in their composition, the Triune God.

CHAPTER IV.

"The Lord Said to My Lord."—Psalm 109 (110).

119.   The Psalms of David have always been considered by Jews and Christians as Messianic prophecies, and they are full of plain allusions to Christ. The one, 109 (110), commonly designated as the Dixit Dominus, from its opening words in the Latin form, seems particularly clear in this respect.

120.   It is not necessary to discuss here the views of those who dispute the Davidic authorship of this sacred song, for all admit that it was written, and was approved by the Jews, long before the birth of Christ.   It is found in the Septuagint, which antedates Christianity by at least two centuries.   It could never have found a place in this translation if it had not been accepted by the Ancient Hebrews as part of their sacred literature and as having the Prophet King for its author.   If this much must be conceded, it is sufficient for our present purpose.

121.   The first verse of this Psalm reads as follows:

"The Lord (Jehova) said to my Lord: sit thou at my right hand; until I make thy enemies thy footstool."   This verse, we think, is the dominant one of the entire Psalm, and it merits our first attention; for, if we are able to fix its true meaning, all that follows can be made to harmonize.

It is evident that two Persons are here dealt with;

and one of them at least is God, for the original
Hebrew text designates Him as Jehova ("Jehova said
to my Lord," etc.) ; a name which the olden Jews
reserved for the Deity alone.

122. There is, in this verse, a strange intermingling of expressions, one indicating absolute equality
and the other dependence. The Second "Lord" is
not said to be inferior. On the contrary, His equality is to be inferred from the phrase "sit thou at
my right hand"; for the rule is, particularly in the
Orient, that the inferior sits below, the superior
above and the equal only "at the right hand."

123. Bethsabee came to her son, King Solomon,
to solicit a favor, and, justly considering her an
equal, he had a throne set for her, so placed that
"she sat on his right hand." 3 (1) Kings 2:19. It
happened frequently in ancient times, that a royal
Father, desiring to share with a son the burthen of
governing, crowned the one so chosen and sat him
upon a throne at his own right hand. Who would
expect, in any Oriental land, or any Occidental one
either, to find a mere subject seated in state, at the
very right hand of his own Emperor or King?

124. And yet, notwithstanding this clear indication of equality between the first Lord and the second one, here referred to, it is the former who is to
subdue the enemies of the latter, and place them
under His feet as a footstool.

125. Must we concede a contradiction here; or
is there any Person known to history, who can possibly satisfy these seemingly conflicting descrip-
tions?

126.   Certain Modern Rabbis, and some critics, have claimed this honor for Abraham; they might as well have claimed it for Job. Great as Abraham was, in faith and in conduct, multitudinous as are his children, both in the flesh and in the spirit, he was no worthier than others, such as Jacob, Isaac, Joseph, Moses, etc., to sit eternally at the right hand of his Creator,[1] and to be named Lord, in the same breath with the great Jehova.

127.   The Patriarch Abraham could not be fairly ranked among the great conquerors, spiritual or temporal (see verses 2, 5, 6), nor as a Judge among nations (verse 6) and, less than all, "a Priest, forever, according to the Order of Melchisedec,"[2] verse 4.

128.   One fact among others shows this attempted explanation to be an afterthought. When the Savior brought up this very text to the Pharisees, Matt. 22:42, *et seq.*, and questioned them concerning it, not one of them suggested that the words applied to Abraham, or in any way challenged the Redeemer's application of them to the Christ.

129.   Equally untenable is the suggestion, offered by some, that it is David who was thus referred to as seated by the Almighty at His own right hand. Such a theory is opposed to all the evidences, furnished by the caption of the Psalm itself, by a con-

---

[1] Saint Paul places Melchisedec higher than Abraham. Hebrews 7:6, 7.

[2] Abraham, himself, Holy Scripture informs us, gave tithes to Melchisedec. Gen. 14:18, 20; Heb. 7:4, *et seq.*

stant tradition and by many express historical declarations, all going to show that this Psalm was written by King David himself. Besides, there is no just reason for supposing that David, any more than Abraham, should be uplifted to an eternal throne of honor and equality, at the very right hand of the awful Jehova.

130. The ancient Romans deified their emperors, for they had a great gallery of gods, and its further extension from time to time could not strike them as in any wise objectionable. But the olden Jews were vastly different in this respect. They worshipped one God, whom they acknowledged as the Creator and Lord of All. Consequently, they held Him in highest esteem, and thought only with deepest awe of His infinite Majesty and Power. They would not, therefore, have attempted to confer upon any mere man, were he king or conqueror, the sacrilegious honor of imputing to him, even metaphorically, anything like an equality with the Deity. And, if one generation had been guilty of so impious a thing, its successors would never have retained the written record of the event as a part of their permanent Sacred Writings.

131. The Psalms are characterized throughout by a spirit of religious reverence. Such literature could not have emanated from a writer or writers who would be capable of seeking to flatter any mere man by declaring him to have been placed by God Himself, on His own right hand, simply because, in a material sense, the man thus honored had "broken kings in the day of his wrath," or was expected in

similar manner "to fill ruins" and to crush heads in the land of many." [1]

132.   It seems also a contradiction to imagine that any resistless warrior, in the temporal order, who had already "broken kings in the day of his wrath," should be invited to sit quietly at the Divine right hand while Jehova Himself was making for this great conqueror, become suddenly passive, a footstool of his enemies. [2]

133.   On the other hand, if the dogmas of the Holy Trinity and of the Incarnation are looked to for a solution of the difficulties which have been suggested in connection with this Psalm, they answer the purpose.   The Messiah, Second Person of the Adorable Trinity, made man, and uniting in His Person both the Divine and the Human Nature, fits perfectly into the first verse of Psalm 109 (110), and does away with every appearance of contradiction between it and the remaining ones.   If we consider His Divinity from this standpoint, it becomes

---

[1] This phrase "crush heads," etc., cannot mean that skulls can be actually broken, with a club, or otherwise.   Verse 6 of Psalm 109 (110) must be read all together; and thus taken it clearly means that Christ shall sit as the Universal Judge ("He shall judge nations") and that, as such Universal Judge, He shall bring to ruin all ungodly nations and generations, and finally cast down and crush all promoters of evil and particularly the leaders in Satan's army upon earth.

[2] It is true that opinion is divided as to whether what is written in verses 5, 6 and 7 of this Psalm applies to Jehova, or to David's Lord.   But if the mighty actions enumerated in these verses be not credited to the "My Lord" of the Psalm, what becomes of the great earthly warrior theory; and what is it that "My Lord" had done theretofore, of a merely secular sort, and for which he should be singled out from all mankind to enjoy the unique and most exalted honor of sitting enthroned forever at the very right hand of God?

evident that Christ was, as God, the equal of the Father, and entitled to sit with Him upon the throne. As God, He had been enthroned on high from all eternity, and had "broken kings in the day of his wrath." From this point of view, therefore, we may give to this phrase last quoted a historical rather than a strictly prophetic application, and find in these words an indication of the divine nature and power of the Son as existing from all eternity. Or we may consider that the Prophet here, as in other places, presents as facts already practically accomplished, the things that God has promised for the future; and this by way of showing how absolutely certain is the Word of God.[1]

134. We have already seen that the expression, "sit thou at my right hand," etc., is figurative and can indicate only that the "Lord" invited thus to sit with Jehova was united, or associated in some manner eternally with the Deity. The Sacred Humanity of the Savior, physically, was not from Eternity; but in the virginal womb of Blessed Mary it became united with the Divinity inseparably and forever; and both natures, thus joined, formed together one Person, Jesus Christ. And when the

---

[1] Another explanation is given by the Fathers of the Church for the occasional use of the past tenses in the description of future events, as also for the presentation of such events as though they were actually occurring in the present. The Prophets were usually enlightened in visions; and it was, therefore, natural for them to record what they saw, as though it were actually taking place, or subsequently as though it had already transpired. Such a course on their part is not unsuggestive of the historical present, with which we are familiar; the past brought back to us imaginatively and described precisely as though it were the present.

Lord Jesus ascended into heaven, He went up just as He was, God and Man; and, as Man, he was placed forever in possession of the throne which, figuratively speaking, He had occupied *as God* from all eternity.

135. Saint Mark,[1] in his Gospel, 16:19, clearly expresses this truth: "And the Lord Jesus, after He had spoken to them, was taken up into heaven, and sitteth on the right hand of God." Saint Peter, in the first of all the Apostolic sermons, gives similar testimony. "Forseeing, he (David) spoke of the resurrection of Christ. This Jesus hath God raised up again, whereof we are all witnesses. Being exalted, therefore, by the right hand of God. For David did not *ascend into heaven;* but he himself said: The Lord said to my Lord, sit thou at my right hand, until I make thine enemies thy footstool." Acts 2:30-35. Saint Paul is to the same effect: "Which he wrought in Christ, raising him up from the dead and setting him at his right hand in the heavenly places." Ephes. 1:20, 21, 22.

136. The Psalmist says *"my* Lord." The possessive pronoun here is a word of importance, and its meaning and purpose must be explained. There is nothing satisfactory, or even plausible, in the suggestion that the "my" of this verse carries no particular message; that David uses the possessive "my" before the second "Lord" only to express the sovereignty of the latter over the whole Jewish nation, king and people. In that view, David should have

---

[1] It is only a blind bigot who will deny to the New Testament all value as interpretative of the Old.

said "Our Lord," for he was writing for his people and not addressing a personal prayer to God. The "my" here must, according to the very nature of the word, express some particular relationship as existing between the Inspired Singer and this "Lord," a relationship that was not one common to all Hebrews. What relationship of this character is there that can be reasonably thought of in this connection, except that, which was to arise in the future from the direct lineal descent of the Messiah, as to His Sacred Humanity, from David himself? [1]

137. The second verse of Psalm 109 (110) also applies clearly to the Messiah: "The Lord will send forth the scepter of thy power out of Zion: rule thou in the midst of thy enemies." The "Scepter (or rod) of thy power" means royal dominion, whether spiritual or secular, and that dominion in this case, originating in Zion (Judea), was to spread: "The Lord shall send forth the Scepter of thy power *out of Zion.*" It was to become universal: "He shall judge *among nations; he* shall fill ruins; he shall crush heads *in the land of many.*" [2] What temporal

[1] "Behold the days come, saith the Lord, and I will raise up to David a just branch, and a king shall reign and shall be wise: and shall execute judgment and justice on earth. In those days Juda shall be saved, and Israel shall dwell confidently: and this is the name they shall call him: The Lord (Jehovah in the Hebrew) Our Just One." Jer. 23:5, 6.
"The book of the Generation of Jesus Christ, the Son of David, the Son of Abraham." Matt. 1:1.

[2] "We have already referred in a footnote to the discussion as to whether verses 5, 6, 7 of our Psalm are directed to Jehovah or to the Messiah. Unless other verses show clearly to the contrary, the "Sit thou at my right hand," of verse 1, must interpret for us the expression of verse 5, "The Lord at thy right hand." It is of no avail to point out that the "My

lord was there of the Jewish nation, or of any other, who, first establishing his reign in Zion,[1] extended it over the nations, so that he became a universal judge [2] or ruler?

138.   That it was a spiritual kingdom which was to be thus begun and extended appears further from the words "rule thou *in the midst* [3] of thy enemies"; words which must mean more than to imply that this Lord was to have in his domains secret or impassive enemies as must be the case with every ruler.   The meaning here is that the enemies among whom the Messiah shall rule, during time, shall be numerous and open, and capable of opposing Him constantly and strongly; and that, until the time when all such are overcome and made His footstool, David's Lord should rule spiritually on earth, subject to and in despite of such open and ever present opposition. How could any mere temporal king "rule" during any length of time under such conditions?   Would he not be expected either to suppress such internal opposition, with promptness, or else resign his throne?

139.   How plainly applicable, on the other hand, are these words to the founding and progress of Christ's kingdom upon earth and to its continued

Lord" of verse 1 is in the Hebrew *Adon,* while in verse 5, *Adonai* is used, and to claim that the latter name belongs in a particular manner to the Deity.   Even were we compelled to grant this distinction between the two names as here used, still, as Christ is God as well as Man, any of the Divine appellatives may be justly applied to Him.

[1] See Isa. 2:3.

[2] See Isa. 2:4.

[3] Not "Over thine enemies," but "in the midst" of them.

experience. How suggestive they are of its con-
quests, despite the persecutions of temporal kings
and governments; of its existence in this world, ever
side by side with the agencies of evil; its persistence
in the face of injustice and oppression.

140. The proposition that this "rule" was to be
spiritual and not secular, finds further support in
the words "in the brightness of thy saints," to be
found in the third verse. We may prefer the Hebrew
text, as we now have it, in this place, "in the brightness of sanctity," or the rendering of the Revised
Version, "in the beauties of holiness"—the result is
not different. In whatever terms the thought may
be correctly expressed, it remains the same. It expresses the holiness of the Messiah and of His followers: and sanctity is not ordinarily a characteristic of earthly conquerors or of the armies they
lead.

141. The fourth verse is very important in its
bearing upon this discussion: "The Lord hath sworn,
and he will not repent; thou art a priest forever,
according to the order of Melchisedec." It will be
observed that, although the Psalm 109 (110) does
not declare, expressly at least, that David's Lord
shall be a king, it does plainly announce his priesthood and its eternal duration.

142. One of the essential functions of the Priesthood is the offering of sacrifice; [1] and it is a fundamental Christian dogma, that Christ Jesus offered
Himself upon Calvary for the sins of men; and that,

[1] "For every high priest is appointed to offer gifts and
sacrifices." Heb. 8:3.

in so doing, He was both High Priest and victim.[1]

143.　We have only a few words concerning Melchisedec in the Old Testament, but these few, rightly studied reveal much: Gen. 14:18, 19, 20.　King of Salem, alien in blood to Abraham, he was nevertheless "the priest of the most high God"; and Abraham recognized him as such, paid tithes to him and took his blessing.　According to the Psalm we are studying, the Messiah was to be a priest according to the order of Melchisedec and this *forever.*[2]

144.　Saint Paul, who was certainly well versed in the sacred learning of his time,[3] guides us in the proper application of these words, "thou art a priest forever," etc.; and for all who are not determined to exclude at all hazards, the Messianic idea from this Psalm his testimony should be conclusive on this subject.　"For this Melchisedec," the Apostle says, in Hebrews, Chap. 7, was "King of Salem, priest of the Most High, who met Abraham returning, Who . . .

[1] "For it was fitting that we should have such a high priest, holy, innocent, undefiled, separated from sinners and made higher than the heavens; who needeth not daily, as other priests, to offer up sacrifices for his own sins and then for the people's: for this he did once, by offering up himself." Heb. 7:26, 27.

[2] Forever, in the Scriptures, has the subordinate meaning, during a life time (Exod. 21:6); but in its broadest, and therefore its preferential sense it expresses the idea of unlimited duration.　Thus we read, in Exod. 3:15, "this is my name forever."　If Christ and his prophetic type were to be priests only for their natural lives, they did not differ in this respect from the Levitical priests, from whom the Apostle Saint Paul has been so careful to distinguish them.　Heb. 7:11, *et seq.*

[3] "And I made progress in the Jews' religion, above many of my equals in my own nation, being more abundantly zealous for the traditions of my fathers." Gal. 1:14.

without father, without mother, without genealogy, without beginning of days nor end of life,[1] but likened unto the Son of God, is a priest forever. . . . And it is yet far more evident; if according to the similitude of Melchisedec, there arise another priest, who is made not according to the law of carnal commandment, but according to the power of an indissoluble life; for he testifieth: Thou art a priest forever according to the order of Melchisedec. . . . By so much is Jesus made surety of a better testament. . . . But this for that he continueth forever, hath an everlasting priesthood. . . . For it is fitting that we have such a high priest, holy, innocent, undefiled, separated from sinners, and made higher than the heavens."

145. The last verse, also, of the Dixit Dominus contributes its support of the Messianic interpretation of the Psalm: "He shall drink of the torrent (or brook) in the way; therefore shall he lift up the head." The word torrent or its equivalent, is used in the Old Testament in various places, to express sorrow, oppression, etc.;[2] and, though other figurative meanings may be claimed for it in other passages of the Old Testament,[3] we are none the less entitled to the benefit to be derived from the interpretation we have preferred, since it is undoubtedly legitimate.

---

[1] That is, all these details are not recorded in Holy Writ.

[2] "When their fury was enkindled against us, perhaps the water had swallowed us up. Our soul hath passed through a torrent," etc. Psa. 103 (104):3, 4, 5. "The sorrows of death surrounded me: and the torrents of iniquity troubled me." Psa. 17 (18):5 (4). Also, II Kings (Sam.) 22:5. "And into what floods of sorrow, now I am." I Mac. 6:11.

[3] See Maas, *Christ in Type and Prophecy,* Vol. II, p. 59.

The word "brook" as used here in certain English translations, may mislead some, for the streams of Palestine, covered by this rendering of the Hebrew word, were larger and deeper than those which we usually designate as brooks; and during rainy periods they become greatly swollen.[1]

146.   The idea of an antecedent humiliation seems apparent in this verse, for the drinking at the torrent implies a lowering of the head in order to reach water.   And this stooping into the torrent is set forth as the cause or occasion for the lifting up that follows "He shall drink of the torrent in the way. *Therefore* shall he lift up the head."   In this view, the passage applies with great clearness to Christ Jesus, the true Messiah, who, unjustly executed as a felon, founded nevertheless a religion which has spread over the entire earth; and Who, having drunk of the bitterness of death, arose gloriously from the dead and is now sitting enthroned eternally in highest Heaven.   This reading has strong New Testament support.   Saint Luke 24:26 asks: "ought not Christ to have suffered these things and *so* have entered into His glory?"   Saint Paul adds his testimony to the same effect.   "He humbled Himself, being obedient unto death, even to the death of the cross. *Wherefore* God hath exalted Him, and hath given Him a name, which is above every name." Phil. 2:8,9.[2]

147.   So far, we have considered principally the internal evidences, as it were, of the Psalm itself;

---

[1] See Hasting's *Bible Dictionary,* Verbo Brook; also Nevin's *Biblical Antiquities,* p. 24; Job 6:15.

[2] See, also, Heb. 2:9.

those which are taken from its own language and construction. The traditional and historical proofs going to show that this sacred song relates to the Christ are very full and complete. The New Testament, regardless of any claim for its inspiration, is a reliable history, and he who denies to it all value as such, must be a fanatic, driven to this position by blind hatred of religion. If the Gospels, the Acts, and the Epistles, be not historical, then we have no histories at all.

148. Three of the Evangelists have related how the Savior, in the presence of the assembled Pharisees, gave to Psalm 109 (110) the Messianic interpretation.

149. "And the Pharisees *being gathered together,* Jesus asked them saying: What think ye of Christ? Whose son is he? And they answer David's. He saith to them: How then doth David in spirit call him Lord, saying: The Lord said to my Lord: Sit thou on my right hand until I make thy enemies thy footstool. If David then call him Lord, how is he his son? And no man was able to answer him a word." Matt. 22:41-46.

150. Saint Mark 12:35-37, and Saint Luke 20:41-44, corroborate the statement of Saint Matthew as given above, and the incident must be considered as historically established.

If this Messianic meaning, thus given by the Savior to Psalm 109 (110) was not the accepted one in His time, why did not some of these proud Pharisees, thus "gathered together," avert their own public discomfiture by disputing His words?

151.   The Gospel, according to Saint Mark, in its last chapter, after describing the resurrection, 16:19, says: "and the Lord Jesus after he had spoken to them was taken up into heaven *and sitteth at the right hand of God.*"

In the first sermon after Pentecost, Saint Peter, Acts 2:34 to 36, makes clear the facts that the Psalm Dixit Dominus does not apply to David and that it did refer to Christ. Preaching of the Savior, this Prince of the Apostles thus expresses himself in this connection: "For David did not ascend into heaven, but he himself said: The Lord said to my Lord, sit thou at my right hand, until I make thy enemies thy footstool," etc.[1]

152.   When Saint Stephen was about to be martyred, he beheld a glorious vision, Acts 7:55: "Jesus standing at the right hand of God. And he said behold I see the heaven opened, and the *Son of Man* standing at the right hand of the Father."

153.   We have already quoted Saint Paul, in the application he makes to Christ, Hebrews, Chap. 7, of the words in our Psalm referring to Melchisedec; which reference he repeats in Heb. 5:5, 6, 10 and 6:20. Again in the same Epistle, 1:3, and 8:1, and 10:12, 13, and in Rom. 8:34, he places Christ on the right hand of the Father; while in 1 Cor. 15:25, in Heb. 1:13 and 10:12, 13, he declares that the Redeemer's reign in Heaven is to last "until he hath all his enemies under his feet."

154.   This strong array of proof from the New

[1] See, also, I Peter 3:22: "Who (Christ) is at the right hand of God."

Testament [1] should hold its own, as proving what was the unquestioned tradition, in this regard, prior to and during the time of Christ upon earth, even were it opposed by the united testimony of the Rabbinical Writers who made their appearance only after the final destruction of Jerusalem. Some of these men, in their hatred of Christ, and in their hostility to Christianity have not scrupled to falsify both the history of their nation, and some of the teachings of their Fathers. When, however, we find, in some of the Rabbinical works unmistakable supports for the interpretation of Psalm 109 (110) which is so plainly and repeatedly set forth in the New Testament, as shown above, we may look upon it as a case confessed and hold it as firmly established that, among the olden Jews, this Psalm was considered as strictly Messianic.

155. In the Targum of Jonathan, the first verse of our Psalm is written: "Jehova said to *his Word*, sit thou at my right hand," etc. This citation, from an ancient and accepted authority, giving *"His Word"* as the equivalent of the term "My Lord," as we now generally find it written in the Dixit Dominus, is destructive of the theories referring the expression of this Psalm to David, or to Abraham, or to any other mere man. As "His Word" (memra) is here used in naming a *Person*, it must have, in the extract last given, the same meaning accorded to it by Saint John in his Gospel, and, likewise by the

---

[1] It is unnecessary to repeat here the several other New Testament passages, on the same line, which have been heretofore given in this article.

Targumists in so many other places, besides the one referred to above.[1]

156.   The Medrasch-Thehillim, on this Psalm, has the following: "The circumstances of the Messiah-King, and his mysteries, are related in the text of the law [2] of the prophets and the hagiographa.   In the text of the hagiographa, for it is said: *Jehova said to my Lord, sit thou at my right*, and the rest up to *thy birth from the womb is like the dew of the morning*.   *Jehova* has sworn and he will not repent: *Thou art a priest forever according to the order of Melchisedec*.   And another verse says: "and lo, one like the Son of Man came with the clouds of heaven, and he came even unto the Ancient of Days; and they presented him before him and he gave him great power, and glory and a kingdom; and all peoples, tribes and tongues shall serve him.   His power is an everlasting power that shall not be taken away; and his kingdom shall not be destroyed."

157.   Medrasch-Thehillim, on Psa. 18:35, and Medrasch-Yalkut, on Psa. 109 (110):1, give the following: "Rabbi Yudan says: In the time to come God the holy, blessed be he, shall place the Messiah-King at his right, for it is written: Sit thou at my right."

158.   R. Mosche-Haddarschan, commenting upon Gen. 18:1: "R. Berahhia in the name of R. Levi began instruction in these words: "It is written: *and you have given me the protection of thy Salvation and thy right hand hath held me up*.   In the time to

[1] See Cruden's *Concordance,* Vo. Word.

[2] By the Law is here meant the Pentateuch.

come, God, the holy, blessed be he, shall place the
Messiah-King at his right; for it is written *Jehova
said to my Lord, sit thou at my right.*"

159.   R. Saadia-Gaon, on Dan. 7:13: *"and they
shall present him before the Ancient of Days as it is
written: Jehova said to my Lord, sit thou at my
right."*

160.   R. Isaac Arama, commenting on Chap. 47
of Genesis: *"Thy birth from the womb is like of the
dew of the morning.* We find no person, no prophet,
whose birth was predicted before his father and
mother had been born, except the Messiah, our Just
one. . . . For, before even the creation of the
Sun, the name of our Messiah was strong and solid
and he was seated at the right hand of God. And
it is said also by the Psalmist: *Sit thou at my right.*
And his throne has been established by grace, and he
is there seated."

161.   R. Obadie Sephorno, on Psalm 109 (110),
has written: "The Sacred Singer composed this
Psalm, in contemplation of the Messiah, and he said:
*Jehova said to my Lord: Sit thou at my right. . . .
Thou art a pontiff forever.* Thou shalt be forever
pontiff-doctor, teaching," etc.[1]

162.   From all the proofs which have been
touched upon above, from the matter and construction of the Psalm itself,[2] and from Christian and

---

[1] The Zohar has similar explanations in many places. See for
above citations from Rabbinical Writers, Drach *De l'Harmonie
entre l'Eglise et la Synagogue.* Vol. II, pp. 50, *et seq.* Also
see Maas, *Christ in Type and Prophecy,* Vol. II, p. 55.

[2] We have abstained from considering, in the body of this
article the paragraph "from the womb, before the day star, I

Jewish tradition it appears clearly that the Dixit Dominus refers to the Messiah and not to any mere earthly king or conqueror. But it may be asked: granted this, does it prove that the Messiah was a divine Person? We may answer that the Psalm rightly interpreted strongly indicates equality between Jehova and David's Lord, for they are pictured to us, seated side by side as Kings upon the same throne. Whatever there may be in the Psalm indicating that it was Jehova who made the Messiah Ruler, etc., cannot take from the showing of equality arising from the seating of the Messiah at Jehova's own right hand. All seeming conflict betweeen the two thoughts must disappear, when we recall the facts that the Messiah is God as well as man, and that, at the Ascension, the Sacred Humanity of Christ, united with His Divinity, went up to sit eternally on the right hand of Jehova.

163. When a proposition is established by a series of proofs, it is not necessary that each of its proofs should be conclusive in itself, as might be a case where but one witness, or but one piece of evidence, is available. Where several different proofs lead to the same conclusion, they interpret and confirm one another. Conceding, therefore, for argument's sake, that, as things are, the Dixit Dominus,

begot thee." This translation is after the Vulgate and the Septuagint: but a wide difference of opinion exists as to what is the proper rendering. To enter effectively into this subject would unduly extend this article, and we find elsewhere proofs enough to sustain our positions. It may be noted, however, that the extract given above, from R. Isaac Arama, tends to show that the Jews considered the paragraph here referred to, as applicable to the eternal begetting of the Son.

standing alone would not be sufficient to establish the fact that the ancient Jews knew of the Trinity, it offers strong corroboration to the other numerous evidences which Holy Scripture furnishes, all going to prove the existence of such knowledge.   Moreover, the Psalm itself is to be interpreted by, or in connection with the passages of this sort, already made use of in this series of articles, and with others to be hereafter quoted.

CHAPTER V.

"Hear, O Israel: The Lord, Our God, the Lord is ONE."—Deut. 6:4.

164. In the earliest days of the Church, Christians and Jews do not seem to have fallen so far apart as they did later. Jewish converts discussed religion with their unconverted brethren and even continued their visits to the Synagogue. The Christian Faith was profiting by this, and was making great progress among the children of Abraham, when the Rabbis, taking alarm, determined to stem this current of conversions. This could be done only by severing the bonds between those who continued in allegiance to the Synagogue and those who had arrayed themselves on the side of Christ. To accomplish this a barrier had to be raised up between Christian and Jew, restricting their intercourse to what was absolutely unavoidable, and making of the remnant of Israel, as it were, a nation apart.

165. Ben Joseph Akiba, a Rabbi who lived during the latter part of the first century after Christ and the earlier portion of the second, may be regarded as the father of this movement, one of the results of which has been the production of the Talmud, which, for modern Jews, has served as a code of laws, spiritual and secular, higher, so far as they could make it so, than the statutes and edicts

of the various countries in which they have been residing.

166.   This Rabbi Akiba, having been an active agent in the sanguinary revolt of the Jews, headed by the false Messiah, Bar-Cochbas, against Hadrian, 131 to 135, A. D., fell eventually into the hands of the Romans, who put him to a painful death. It is declared that, as his flesh was being torn from his bones, and until his last breath, he recited aloud the opening words of what Jews call the *Shema:* "Hear O Israel, Jehova, Our Lord, Jehova is one." Deut. 6:4.

167.   Since Akiba's time, these words have been the cry, as it were, of Modern Judaism, as well as of Gentile Unitarianism, in their warfare against the dogma of the Holy Trinity. The Talmud opens with them, and they are recited frequently and reverently by devout Jews.

168.   But the claim of Unitarianism that this Scriptural passage is a plain proclamation of a Divine Unity, so absolute as to positively exclude the idea of the Trinity, is without just foundation. If the sacred words are not to be construed as favoring Trinitarianism, then they are without any significance whatsoever in this regard.

169.   Both the Douay and the King James Version give the following as the English of this text, Deut. 6:4: "Hear, O, Israel: The Lord, our God is one Lord." This is not a close translation of the Vulgate, which is nearer to the Hebrew and if put into English rigorously would read: "Hear, O Israel: The Lord, our God, the Lord is One." [1]

[1] "Audi Israel, Dominus, Deus Noster, Dominus Unus est."

170. The original Hebrew does not of itself strictly support even the Vulgate rendition, for in that original form we find the *"is"* omitted. A strictly literal translation of the Hebrew would give us: "Jehova, Our Gods (Elohenu), Jehova, One."

171. Therefore, the demand might be as well made to supply the omitted verb of the Hebrew text with the plural "are" instead of with the singular "is"; and this would render the "Hear, O Israel," etc., a manifest exposition of the dogma of the Trinity. Under such conditions it is a decided begging of the question, to supply a singular verb, where there is none in the original, and then to claim as established a result which has no other base than the very word inserted.

172. Furthermore, even if we yield this point, and consent to the insertion in question, namely, "is" instead of "are," the cause of Unitarianism is not advanced; for the plurality of Divine Persons, which Trinitarianism proclaims, is inherent in the Unity of the Divinity. Indeed it should perhaps be granted that the Unity, in Divinity, of the Three Divine Persons is so complete as to exclude the observance, in this important passage, of the grammatical rule or usage, which gives to a verb its plural form, by preference, where, otherwise, it might as well be placed in one number as in the other. We find a similar departure, in this same connection, from the ordinary rule of grammar, and the consequent use of singular verbs repeatedly, when their subject is *Elohim,* the Divine Name in its plural form. Indeed, in the three successive repetitions of the Almighty's name which

are found in the "Hear, O Israel," etc., this same plural form *Elohim* is included in one of its variations, *Elohenu*.

173. But, if the intention was here to solemnly proclaim a Divine Unity, so absolute as to even exclude the idea of a plurality of Divine Persons, why not, for so grave a purpose, employ language and a form of expression so simple as to preclude misunderstanding? Surely, the idea of His being Israel's God, and one only, would have been sufficiently and more clearly stated by the words "Jehova, Our God, is One." Why the triple repetition here of the Divine name, in forms not all alike, which, from the point of view of Unitarianism, must introduce confusion, where clearness was so essential? And, if it be, as some contend, that this solemn pronouncement was given forth by the Almighty as a particular condemnation of Trinitarianism, how is it that the inspired writer was permitted to thus furnish to Trinitarians, in this very passage, justification for their belief; by the *triple* repetition of the Divine Name, by the use of the plural form *Elohenu*, and by the omission of the verb?

174. It is undoubtedly true that this passage deals in an especial manner with the personal nature of God. It could not have been intended to announce merely the already acknowledged fact that Jehova is God, or that He was Israel's God; for the capital thought of the passage is expressed by the word ONE. In the verse in question, all that goes before the term ONE, but leads directly up to this culmination, the expression of the Unity of God.

But, from the Unitarian point of view, what great purpose is there for this passage to serve? The old pagans, in this very same sense, regarded Jupiter as one individual God, and Juno as one individual goddess; but they saw no need, in either case, to specially proclaim these facts, which they considered as self-evident. And, if the meaning of Deut. 6:4, is merely to declare that Jehova is a personal, individual divine Being, as Jupiter and Juno, each of them, were once supposed to be, why should the One, true God, inspire a proclamation, so needless, of his own individual being and put that proclamation into a form so solemn and impressive?[1] This sentence, therefore, must have been intended for some deeper and more useful purpose than to announce, simply, that Jehova was one God, as Jupiter was supposed, by deluded heathens, to be one. It was designed to express some special characteristic inherent in the very Unity of Jehova, which did not and could not exist in connection with the unity of Jupiter.

175. If the proposition last laid down be true, it follows reasonably that there must be connected with the Unity of Jehova, or we might say there is within it, some feature, or characteristic, rendering it essentially different from all other unities, hence absolutely unique. And it may be claimed further that the mission of the HEAR, O ISRAEL is to proclaim this mystery, whatever it may be.

---

[1] Not only does the verse in question, Deut. 6:4, concern the most exalted of all subjects, Jehova, Himself, and not only is its language and form of expression most impressive, but we find it introduced by this striking appeal to the Nation: "Hear, O Israel."

176. Now, what feature, or characteristic, can there be inherent in the divine Unity in such a manner as to make it unique and different from any other Unity whatsoever, and yet, at the same time, without impairing its integrity in the least degree?

177. The Unitarian can give no answer to this question; since his contention is for a divine unity that is not in fact unique; that is unity only in the general acceptation of the term, and as expressive of mere individuality, the "state of oneness," and nothing more.

178. On the other hand the dogma of the Holy Trinity presents to us the Unity of God as different from and unlike all other unities. If accepted, that dogma puts a sufficient motive and reason behind the "Hear, O Israel," and makes it a dignified and solemn indication of a great truth, the unique Unity of the Godhead, which alone discloses a plurality of Persons in a Unity of Being.

179. In the interpretation of a work, such as Holy Scripture, every word has its value, and every peculiarity of construction is entitled to close consideration. While words, and phrases and whole sentences may indeed be corrupted, by interpolation or otherwise, the presumption is in favor always of the honesty of the text. The striking expression, "Jehova, our Gods, Jehova, One" if appearing originally in our own language, would naturally suggest some strange combination of unity and plurality. A study of the words composing it would justify a train of thought like the following: The name

Jehova, as an individual name, of itself suggests unity, or oneness: therefore, certainly, the mere idea of absolute divine Unity would find clearer expression in the words "Jehova, One," standing for "Jehova is One." And, since the Unity of God is sufficiently expressed without it, the term *Elohenu* in the text is there to disclose some other idea, closely connected with the idea set forth by the other words, but still additional.

180. *Elohim* is a word of plural form; yet, despite its plurality, it is often applied in Holy Scripture to the One God. Its difference, therefore, in this connection, from the name *Jehova* lies, in its grammatical number. Under such circumstances, may it not be said that *Elohenu* is used here because of its being a divine name in plural form, and for the purpose of indicating that there is in God, plurality and Unity combined; plurality of Persons, with unity of Being? Finally, we may view the second Jehova of the passage, as an additional precaution, a restriction upon and further explanation of the *Elohenu,* to prevent any polytheistic interpretation; in fact, as a reassertion of the divine Unity. And we may see, in this passage the same meaning that it would convey, if, in place of the terms of the text, these three words had been written in succession Unity, plurality, unity.

181. This does not conflict with the view that the name of God is thrice repeated in this passage, one time for each of the three divine Persons: on the contrary, it confirms it. It is perfectly legitimate to employ a single form of speech, for the expression of

different though germane ideas, in connection with the same subject.

182. We find, in the Old Testament, other passages wherein the name of God is thrice mentioned, or referred to, in immediate succession, and which may be regarded as in line with Deut. 6:4, *et seq.*:

"The Lord bless thee and keep thee,

"The Lord shew his face to thee, and have mercy on thee,

"The Lord turn his countenance to thee and give thee peace." Num. 6:24, 25, 26.

183. And, in Jos. 22:22, is "The Lord the most mighty God, the Lord," etc.; which in the original Hebrew is more striking and more illustrative of our present subject—*el, Elohim, Jehova.*[1]

184. In Isa. 6:1, 2, 3, *et seq.*, the Prophet describes his vision of the Lord, with two attending seraphim; and the cry of the latter was, verse 3, "Holy, Holy, Holy, Lord God of Sabaoth; all the earth is full of his glory." Adjectives are often used as nouns or names in the Sacred Writings. Indeed, in olden times, individuals were often designated by adjectives, or by nouns used as such, indicative of striking characteristics, for which they were noted. The baptismal names, still in favor, were, many of them originally mere descriptive adjectives.

---

[1] Nahum 1:2 need not be dwelt upon. Verse 3 of this chapter must go with verse 2: and between the two verses the divine name is mentioned five times, in immediate succession. If it be insisted, however, that in verse 2, God is mentioned triply in His quality as an Avenger, then the verse falls in line with the quotations given above.

God, Himself, is often designated by some adjective expressive of a divine attribute: the Almighty, the Omnipotent; the Eternal, the Allwise, etc. Since holiness [1] is a divine attribute, as well as omnipotence, etc., there is no more reason why the adjective "Holy," as found, thrice repeated, in Isa. 6:3,[2] should not be made, like the other adjectives mentioned above, to do duty as a divine name. Such an interpretation would place Isa. 6:3, in close accord with Deut. 6:4, and make one as it were the equivalent of the other.[3]

185.   It is true that triple repetitions are occasionally found elsewhere in the Old Testament and in other connections, but these others occur in passages which deal with lesser and finite things, and not with God and His Nature. In one class of cases no extraordinary care in expression was demanded and liberty might be taken for poetical or other literary effect; but in the passages we are now studying particularly, the subject was God and His Nature, and every word used called for the strictest scrutiny in

---

[1] "Be ye holy, because I, the Lord, thy God, am holy." Levit. 19:2.

[2] Saint John, in the Apocalypse (Revelations) 4:8, also tells of "the four living creatures" that "rested not day or night," saying "Holy, holy, holy, Lord God Almighty, who was, who is and who is to come."

[3] It is not impossible that the "holy" three times repeated, of Isa. 6:3, is a species of epizeuxis, for the sake of emphasis, or else an oriental circumlocution for the superlative. But the text itself of this passage is not more in favor of either of the explanations just mentioned than of the one defended in the body of this article; and the support which the Trinitarian interpretation draws from other kindred passages in the Old Testament is very strong.

order to avoid the obscuring of a great and fundamental religious truth.[1]

186. But it is not essential, in order to find in
Isa. 6:3, a Trinitarian meaning, to insist that this
"Holy, Holy, Holy," of the Prophet is a triple repe-
tition of the divine Name. Many eminent Christian
Writers [2] regard this word "holy," here employed,
as an exclamation of praise, three times repeated in
honor of and to designate the Three Persons of the
Holy Trinity.

187. It may surprise some to learn that the interpretations herein defended are not without support from Jewish writers.

"Behhai, one of the most celebrated of those Rabbins who flourished with such renown in Spain during
the thirteenth century, says in his commentary, following tradition, that Moses commands in this text
(Deut. 6:4) the belief that the three general attributes of the Divinity are united in one; namely, the
Eternity, the Wisdom, the Prudence." [3]

188. R. Aron, surnamed the Great, Chief of the
Babylonian Academy (prior to the eleventh century)
in his work on Punctuation says:

"No man, whatever may be his efforts, can form a

---

[1] The "Earth, earth, earth," of Jer. 22:29, and Ezechiel's
(21:27) "iniquity, iniquity, iniquity," are mere repetitions for
literary effect and they give rise to no confusion of any sort.
The repetitions in Jer. 7:4 may be not unreasonably regarded
as an error in copying, and, in any event, it falls under what
has just been said with regard to Jer. 22:29 and Ezechiel
(21:27).

[2] Cf. Petav. de Trin. I, II, Chap. 7.

[3] Chevalier P. B. L. Drach: *De l'Harmonie entre l'Eglise et
la Synagogue,* Vol. I, p. 310.

true idea of the triple number in the *manner of being*, in the *essence* of God; in this regard close your mouth and do not seek to explain this natural disposition of His being. It is to announce this sublime mystery that, in this verse: "Hear, O Israel, Jehova, Elohenu, Jehova, One,' the last vowel is a Kametz. For *Kametz* signifies *close*, as if the text said close your mouth and do not speak it."

189. The Zohar, on Deuteronomy, fol. 126, cols. 501, 502, has the following:

"Hear, O Israel, etc., Jehova, Principle of all things, by the light of the Ancient,[1] and it is He who is called the Father.

"Elohenu, the valley, from which are the sources of the stream that flows toward all.

"Jehova (the second of the verse) branches of the tree, perfection of the roots."

The same work (Zohar) on the Book of Numbers, fol. 77, col. 307, contains the following: "He said furthermore: There are *two*, to which *one* unites itself; and being *three*, they are but *one:* These two are the two Jehova of the verse, *Hear, O Israel. Elohenu* joins itself to them. . . . And, as they are joined together, they are one in a *unity which is unique.*"

190. Other passages, to the same effect, from the Zohar, might be added here, but to do so would be to lengthen this chapter unduly.[2] It matters not when

[1] "I beheld, therefore, in the vision of the night, and lo, one like the Son of Man came with the clouds of heaven, and he came even unto the *Ancient of Days:* and they presented him, before him." Dan. 7:13.

[2] "More distinct, however, is the doctrine of the Trinity. On

or how this book originated, it is certainly a work
written by a Jew, or Jews, and for Jews. It dates at
the least from the beginning of the fourteenth century, and it has been accepted and venerated during
many generations, by the dispersed communities of
Israel. Therefore, it served well to support the conclusion that, if the Messiah, for whom the unconverted Children of Abraham are still sighing so
vainly, had appeared as they had brought themselves to expect, in the guise of a great conqueror,
and had he led them to the hoped for subjugation of
the entire Gentile world, they would have found
ample warrant, in the "Hear, O Israel" and in other
parts of their Sacred Writings, and in their Rabbinical books, to justify them in regarding their
great King and universal Conqueror as the true Son
of the Most High God.[1]

191.   There are two kinds of unity that may find

Deut. 6:4, where Jehova occurs first, then Elohenu, and then
again Jehova, we are told 'The voice, though one, consists of
three elements, fire (*i. e.,* warmth), air (*i. e.,* breath) and
water (*i. e.,* humidity), yet all three are one in the mystery
of the voice and can only be one. Thus also Jehova, Elohenu,
Jehova constitute one—three forms which are one' (Zohar, ii
43: compare iii, 65). Discussing the thrice holy in Isaiah, VI,
3, one codex of the Zohar had the following remark: 'The first
holy denotes the Holy Father, the second the Holy Son, and
the third the Holy Ghost' (Comp. Galatinus De Arcacanis
Cathol., lib. ii, c. p. 31: Wolf, *Bibliotheca Hebraica,* I, 1136."
Rev. L. Ginsburg, LL. D., in *Encyclopædia Britannica,* Vo.
Kabbalah.

[1] When, during the seventeenth century, Sabbatai Zebi appeared as a pseudo-Messiah, he proclaimed himself the Son of
God, first-begotten, made flesh to redeem Israel. And his
claims as such were, for a time, universally recognized among
the Jews. *The Messiah Idea in Jewish History,* by Julius H.
Greenstone, Ph. D., pp. 213, *et seq.*

expression in the word *one*. The term suggests, in the first place, a unity which may be designated simple, whenever there is not any aggregation of units existing, or considered. Further, it serves to express a unity, which we may call aggregate, when it is composed, or made up of two or more units or individuals. Thus, the earth is one, in the simple sense, for it is not a collection of terrestrial orbs, considered or dealt with as an aggregate. Our great American Republic, on the other hand, is also *one*, though it be composed of a number of States, all of them republican, likewise, in their forms of government.

192. The idea of simple unity, as explained above, and which is more closely represented in English by the form "an only" is expressed in Hebrew by a word of four letters, יָחִיד, adjective and substantive, with the definition "only, only one, solitary." See Hebrew and English Lexicon of the Old Testament, by Francis Brown, S. R. Driver and C. A. Briggs, p. 402. We have an example of the use of this word of four letters in Zach. 12:10: "And they shall look upon me whom they have pierced; and they shall mourn for him as one mourneth for an only (one) son." See, also, Gen. 21:2; Amos 8:10; Prov. 4:3; Psa. 21 (22):21; 34 (35):17; 24 (25):16, etc. In all the range of Holy Scripture this Hebrew word of four letters is never once applied to Jehova, or used in connection with Him.[1]

193. The unity, however, which is or may be ag-

---

[1] *Genesis, with a Talmudic Commentary,* Paul Isaac Hershon, p. 466; T. N. b.

gregate, or which at all events does not exclude the idea of aggregation or composition, is represented in the Hebrew Old Testament by a word of three letters, אֶחָד. This word is used, for instance, in Ezek. 37:19, where there is question of laying sticks together in the hand and making of them one; and in Gen. 1:15, "there was evening and morning, one day."

194.   In the "Hear, O Israel," the Sacred Writer has used the word last considered, of three letters, to express the divine unity (one) and not the more positive or absolute word, composed of four letters, described above.

195.   A circumstance that is worthy of consideration here is that the two vowel marks placed under the word *one,* as the latter is found in the Hebrew of Deut. 6:4, seem plainly suggestive of the Trinity. The first is Segol (∵) : three dots, two above and one below.   The second is Kametz (T), like the Greek letter tau, or our own twentieth letter, written as a capital, and in its simplest form, with two straight strokes.   This second vowel mark, Kametz, may be regarded as formed of the three dots of the Segol, united into one symbol, by the use of two lines ; one across uniting the upper dots, and a second connecting the lower by a line running up.

196.   Thus, in the vowel marks which the Jews employ in connection with the word *one,* as found in this passage, there appears a plain indication of the Trinity ; the first, Segol, by its three distinct dots, standing for the three divine Persons, and the second, Kametz, showing these three united in One.

197.   Conceding that vowel marks, as now employed in writing the Hebrew, were not used until some centuries after Christ; it is known that the Rabbinical Writers were constantly seeking mystical meanings everywhere; and that they likewise endeavored to express in occult ways some of their teachings, so as to hide them carefully from Christians, and doubtless also from the ignorant or rash among their own nation.

198.   This spirit, or rather these tendencies, may have influenced, to some extent, the adoption, or the development of the Hebrew system of vowel marks. If the Ancient Synagogue recognized the dogma of the Holy Trinity, it is not improbable that the more learned and the Chiefs among the Rabbis, in the times of the introduction of vowel marks into the Hebrew, aware of this ancestral tradition, attached vowel marks to the important word *one* in the Schema, that would express the truth for the initiated, while concealing it from others.   Many passages are to be found scattered through the Rabbinical writings, in which reference is made, more or less veiled but discernible, to the sacred mystery of the Trinity of God.   There is no reason, therefore, why we should not see, in the vowel marks that have been assigned to the Hebrew word *"One,"* as now written in Deut. 6:4, a veiled expression of this same great dogma.

199.   This explanation is supported by the fact that, in ancient manuscripts of the Targums, the name of Jehova is found replaced with three points

or dots, and sometimes with three yods,[1] with, in either case, the three-armed, tau-shaped Kametz placed just beneath.[2] In some instances, in these same old manscripts, evidently for the purpose of emphasizing the idea of plurality embraced in Unity, a circle is drawn around the points and marks; all to represent the ineffable Name.

200. All doubt should disappear upon this point, when we consider the facts, that, when, in later days, Christians began to acquaint themselves with the Rabbinical writings, the Rabbis dropped out in their copies and writings, and particularly in the books of prayer, one of the three yods, leaving two only, with the *cametz* still beneath, to stand for the divine Name.[3] That this was a device to further conceal the great truth which we are considering is shown not only by the condition, as we have seen, of some of the older manuscripts, particularly of the Paraphrases, but also by frequent references in the Zohar to "the three yods" of the Sacred Name.

201. By all of the above, the following propositions seem proven clearly:

1. The "Hear, O Israel," etc., of Deut. 6:4, is not a proclamation of the Unitarian belief, with regard to the Unity of God.

---

[1] Yod: tenth letter of the Hebrew alphabet, not unlike in appearance our comma mark.

[2] Chevalier Drach, *De l'Harmonie entre l'Eglise et la Synagogue*, Vol. I, p. 309. Buxtorfii: dissert de Nominib. Dei Hebr., No. 28.

[3] Drach, *De l'Harmonie entre l'Eglise et la Synagogue*, Vol. I, p. 367.

2.   It is upon its very face a divine announcement of the great mystery of the Trinity.

3.   It was accepted in the latter sense by the Olden Jews, and secretly by many, if not all, of the Chiefs among modern ones.

CHAPTER VI.

"THE WORD OF JEHOVA."

202. THE Gospel, according to Saint John, begins with these expressive sentences:

"In the beginning was the Word, and the Word was with God, and the Word was God. The same was in the beginning with God. All things were made by Him; and without Him was made nothing that was made."

And again, verse 14, the same Evangelist says:

"And the Word was made flesh and dwelt among us (and we saw His glory, the glory as it were of the only begotten of the Father), full of grace and truth."

203. The passages quoted above give a clear statement of the existence of the Word from all Eternity, as, also, of His divine nature and of His Incarnation. They likewise show the plurality of Persons existing in God.

204. In the above quotation, the Inspired Writer uses "the Word" (Logos) with certainty and assurance, and as a term which his contemporaries would understand. Indeed, this term, or its equivalents, used nominally, frequently appears in the Old Testament, and a question naturally suggests itself, whether the numerous texts in the Older Scriptures, wherein "the Word of Jehova," or any of its substitutes, is mentioned, are in accord with the testi-

mony given by Saint John in regard to the divine
nature of the Word.

205. Logos, or Word, has a narrower sense, by
which it refers to any mere spoken or written sign
of a particular conception or thought; but it is not
in this restricted sense that the term is to be taken,
when found in ancient sacred or philosophical literature. Therein it stands, not only for speech,[1] as the
means by which the human mind reveals its thoughts
or concepts, but also for those thoughts or concepts
themselves, as thus revealed by speech. If thoughts
thus manifested, and preserved, are wise, the speech
or language in which they are expressed may be
called Wisdom; hence Logos and Sophia, Word and
Wisdom are to a certain extent synonymous.[2]

206. But the Word or Wisdom of ancient believers and thinkers was not simple, inactive, unliving
speech. It stood for the divine Reason, manifesting
itself in external works, and, also necessarily, for the
divine Will accomplishing its purposes in external
creation. In other words, it was the Supreme Being,
in some way creating and governing; and the question is, whether that divine action and control were
considered as immediate or mediate.

207. We need not just now concern ourselves
with the discussions, on this subject, among the olden
Greek philosophers, who, in all probability, originally derived from the Hebrews the conception of the

---

[1] "Who sendeth forth his Speech to the earth; his Word
runneth swiftly." Psa. 147:15.

[2] "The Word of God on high is the fountain of Wisdom,
and her ways are everlasting commandments." Eccles.
(Sirach) 1:5.

Word or Logos; and who, in their speculations and
debates, made it assume so many varied shapes. Nor
will the writings of Philo assist us here, for they
form no part of the sacred literature of Israel, and
the value of his testimony as to the ancient beliefs of
his people, in this regard, is impaired by the fact that
he was in disposition and training as much of a
Greek as of a Jew. Moreover, as a Platonist, his
motive was, not so much to record what the Hebrew people believed with regard to the Word, as to
reconcile, or harmonize those beliefs with the teachings of his Greek master.

208. The Old Testament is, therefore, the source
to which we must look, principally at least, for information upon the subject we have in hand: and our
purpose is to prove from its sacred pages, that the
Word or Wisdom of God is a personal Being; that
He is not a mere creature, representing or acting for
Jehova; that He is now in fact, what He has been
from all eternity in the divine Mind and purpose,
namely, Creator and Creature; in other words, God
and Man—Christ, Jesus.

209. It is worthy of notice that, in Genesis, God
is represented as accomplishing the work of creation
by speaking: "And God *said*, let there be light," etc.
This form of expression, found in Gen. 1:3, 6, 9, 11,
etc., may or may not have been intended to indicate
the participation of the Word in the constitution of
the universe. Some writers consider that it does
furnish such indication; and, while, if standing alone,
this feature of the Genetic history would not prove
our proposition, it nevertheless may serve as cor-

roborative evidence.   Had He so desired, the Almighty could have brought all created things into being by the simple operation of His Will; and there was no absolute necessity that His will, thus operating, should have found expression in actual words. But, accepting the Logos, or Sophia, as suggestive of Speech, in the highest sense of the term, and as such used metonymically as one of the divine names, we may take the form of expression, "and God said," etc., so often used in the first chapter of Genesis, as intimating in another way the fact that God, "by His Word," made the Universe.

210.   In searching the Old Testament for proofs of belief in the Holy Trinity, we should be ready to take into consideration every character of evidence, obscure as well as clear, figurative as well as literal; and our final conclusion should be arrived at only after a careful study of the entire case.   Many concurring witnesses may together prove, beyond all doubt, a particular chain of facts, which no one of them, taken separately, is capable of establishing sufficiently.   And, as the different witnesses, in the same cause, use ordinarily different forms of words or different methods of expression in testifying to the same facts, we should expect to find, in the Scriptures, the same truth stated and restated in a variety of ways.

211.   We have quoted above the language of Saint John relative to the Word and seen how manifest is its application to the Savior.   The Old Testament also speaks often of "the Word of Jehova"; and, while in some passages this expression may refer to

speech in its narrower and more literal sense, in others it seems plainly to convey the same idea as the one formulated, as we have seen, by the holy Evangelist.

212.   In I Kings (I Samuel), Chap. 3, we read of the Lord's calling, during the night, to the child Samuel, and of the boy's imagining, at first, that it was the voice of Heli; for (verse 7), "Samuel did not yet know the Lord, neither had the *Word* of God been revealed to him."

In the same book, Chap. 15, verses 11, 12: "And the *Word* of the Lord came to Samuel saying: It repenteth *Me* that *I* have made Saul king; for he hath forsaken *Me* and hath not executed *My* commandments."

In Psa. 32 (33):6: "By the *Word* of the Lord the heavens were established, and the power of them by *the Spirit of His mouth.*"

Psa. 106 (107):20: "He sent His *Word* and healed them, and delivered them from their destructions."

Psa. 147:15: "Who (God) sendeth forth His *Speech* to the earth, His *Word* runneth swiftly."

Wisdom 9:1: "God of my fathers and Lord of Mercy, who hast made all things with Thy *Word.*"

Wisdom 18:15: "Thy *Almighty Word* leapt down from heaven from Thy royal throne."

Isa. 55:11: "So shall My *Word* be, which shall go forth from My mouth; it shall not return to Me void, but *it shall do* whatsoever I please and shall *prosper the things for which I sent* it."

213.   Numerous as are the passages above given, and clear as they are in themselves to unhostile minds,

they are originally from the Hebrew or Greek texts; and, in their interpretation, we should accept the aid of the Aramaic version or versions, known as the Targums, or Paraphrases, in which the form "Word of Jehova" is used still more frequently than in either the Hebrew or the Greek versions, and more plainly as indicating the Messiah.

214. These Targums, or Paraphrases, were translations of the books of the Old Testament into Aramaic, which became the current language of the Jews, after the ancient Hebrew had fallen into disuse among the people, in consequence of their long sojourn as captives in the Babylonian Empire. Several of these translations have been lost entirely, and those remaining are much corrupted; but those we still possess, where not corrupted, are entitled to at least the same consideration as the Hebrew originals. They are repetitions of the Sacred Text in a new language, but they were also repetitions by and for the same people; and we can rightfully expect to find faithfully mirrored in them interpretations of Holy Writ accepted by the Children of Israel, before the Advent of Christ.

215. It would too greatly extend this article to attempt the reproduction here of all passages in the Targums, wherein *Memra*, or "the *Word*," is referred to as a divine Actor, or is used in places or in connections going to show that it applies to the Messiah, recognized as a divine Person. We will here content ourselves with the testimony of one, who, though not a modern critic, was a faithful student of the Scriptures. We refer to Alexander Cruden, who,

in his well-known Concordance, under the heading
Word, gives the following brief statement, in this
connection:

216. "The Chaldee Paraphrasts, the most ancient Jewish writers extant, generally make use of
the word *Memra*, which signifies the *Word* in those
places where Moses puts the name Jehova. And it is
generally thought, that, under this term, the Paraphrasts would intimate the Son of God, the Second
Person of the Trinity. Now their testimony is so
much the more considerable as having lived before
Christ, or at the time of Christ, they are irrefragible
witnesses of the sentiments of their nation concerning
this article, since their Targum, or Explication, has
always been, and still is, in universal esteem among
the Jews. And, as they ascribe to *Memra* all the attributes of the Deity, it is concluded from thence,
that they believed the divinity of the *Word*.

217. "They say it was the *Memra*, or the *Word*,
which created the world; which appeared to Moses on
Mount Sinai; which gave him the law; which spoke to
him face to face; which brought Israel out of Egypt;
which marched before the people; which wrought all
those miracles which are recorded in the book of
Exodus. It was the same Word that appeared to
Abraham in the plain of Mamre; that was seen of
Jacob at Bethel, to whom Jacob made his vow, and
acknowledged as God, Gen. 28:20. 'If God will be
with me, and will keep me in this way that I go, etc.,
then shall the Lord be my God.' " [1]

[1] Any reader interested to follow more fully this line of investigation and to verify the statement, foregoing, from Cru-

218.   We have already seen, in this connection,
that the terms *Word* and *Wisdom* may be held as
synonymous.   It will serve our purpose, therefore,
to show that the latter, as well as the former, is frequently used, in the Old Testament, in a personified
sense, and is presented as occupying the divine relation toward the world and particularly toward men.
We quote some of the passages in which the term
Wisdom is thus used.

219.   Prov. 3:19, 20: "The Lord by Wisdom hath
founded the earth, hath established the heavens by
prudence.   By His Wisdom the depths have broken
out, and the clouds grow thick with dew."

220.   Same, 8:22, *et seq.*: "The Lord possessed
me (Wisdom) in the beginning of his ways before he
made anything from the beginning.   I was set up
from eternity, and of old before the earth was made.
The depths were not as yet, *and I was already conceived*, neither had the fountains of water as yet
sprung out.   The mountains, with their huge bulk

den's *Concordance* may do so, by consulting the following
principal passages from the Pentateuch, and substituting in
each, for Jehova—or the Lord as the divine name Jehova is
usually rendered in English texts—the name Memra or the
Word.   This list is from the work of Chevalier P. B. L. Drach,
De l'Harmonie entre l'Eglise et la Synagogue, Vol. II, p. 404,
and is as follows:
   "Gen. 1:27, 28; 3:8, 9, 22, 23; 5:24; 6:36; 8:21; 15:6; 17:7;
18:1; 19:24; 20:21, 22; 21:33; 22:4, 14; 26:11, 30; 28:20, 21;
30:22; 31:48, 49; 35:9; 38:25; 48:21.
   "Exod. 2:25; 3:14; 14:9, 15; 16:8; 19:3 (ed. de Ximenes),
17; 20:1; 29:43; 32:20, 21, 22.
   "Lev. 24:12; 26:11, 30, 46.
   "Num. 9:18, 23; 11:20; 14:9; 22:18; 23:21; 24:6, 13.
   "Deut. 1:27, 30, 32, 43; 2:7; 3:12; 4:24, 32, 33, 36, 37; 5:5;
9:3, 18, 23, 24, 26; 18:16, 19; 20:1; 26:14; 27:17, 18; 31:6, 8;
32:48; 33:2, 7."

had not yet been established; before the hills *I was brought forth;* He had not yet made the earth, nor the rivers, nor the poles of the world. When he prepared the heavens I was present; When with a certain law and compass he enclosed the depths; When he established the sky above, and poised the fountains of waters; When he compassed the sea with its bounds, and set a law to the waters that they should not pass their limits; When he balanced the foundations of the earth I was with him in the forming of all things; and was delighted every day playing before Him at all times; playing in the world, and my delights were to be with the children of men. . . . He that shall find me shall find life and shall have salvation from the Lord; but he that shall sin against me shall hurt his own soul. All that hate Me love death."

221. Wisdom 7:24 to 27: "For Wisdom is more active than all active things; and reacheth everywhere by reason of her purity. *She is a vapor of the power of God,* and a certain *pure emanation of the glory of the Almighty God;* and, therefore, no defiled thing cometh into her. For she is the brightness of eternal life and the unspotted mirror of God's majesty, and the image of his goodness."

Wisdom 9:4: "Give me Wisdom *that sitteth by Thy throne,* and cast me not off from among thy children."

Eccles. (Sirach) 1:1: "All Wisdom is from the Lord God, and hath been always with him, and is before all time."

222. In the same book (Eccles. 1:4, 5), Wisdom

and the Word of God are presented to us as one: "Wisdom hath been created before all things, and the understanding of prudence from everlasting. The Word of God on high is the fountain of Wisdom and her ways are everlasting commandments."

223. Chapter 24 of Ecclesiasticus is too long to be reproduced here, but it is difficult for an unbiased reader to peruse it, in its entirety, without admitting that there is strong reason for concluding that therein Wisdom is spoken of as a distinct Being and identical with the Messiah, the "Mighty King," Who was to come into this world as a son or direct descendant of David.

224. In regard to the present issue, it does not destroy the evidential value of the passages just quoted from the Old Testament, or of those referred to in the Targums, to show that in certain places, in both these works, Wisdom and Word are occasionally used in such a way as to make it plain that they do not refer to the Deity. Any word having various meanings is of necessity liable to be variously employed. Even the word God is used in different senses, in Holy Scripture and elsewhere; but this affords no reason for refusing to recognize it as a special name of the Almighty, Himself, in a multitude of other passages, in the same works, where evidently it can have no other signification.

225. The Zohar applies the term Wisdom to God, and uses the term Word for the same purpose. For instance, dealing with the first verse of Genesis, it employs the following language, fol. 15, col. 58: "In the Beginning (Bereschit) Mystery of the *Wisdom.* In

the Beginning, this is the *Word*, which corresponds with the *Degree of Wisdom*, it is called 'Reschit.' " By "Degrees" as used here and elsewhere in the Zohar, are meant Degrees of God; or, in other words, the divine Hypostases, or Persons. This may be seen by reference, among other things, to the paraphrase, in the work last quoted from, of the Psalm, "Dixit Dominus," as follows: "The first Degree said to the second Degree, sit thou at My right hand." [1]

226. We may conclude this article by recurring to the texts with which it opens, taken from the Gospel of Saint John. This Evangelist was a Hebrew and a man of learning. Without entering just now into the question of the correctness of his conclusion as to the Lord Jesus being the Word made flesh, the statement of Saint John, made by way of premise, is valuable in the present discussion, as a proof of the generally accepted belief of the people, in his time, that "in the beginning was the Word and the Word was God."

---

[1] Drach, *De l'Harmonie entre l'Eglise et la Synagogue,* Vol. 1, p. 417, note (c). Zohar (Gen., fol. 35, col. 139). Same 1, p. 417, note (c).

CHAPTER VII.

"LET US MAKE MAN."—GEN. 1:25.

227. WE HAVE studied, heretofore, the strange intermingling of plural and singular, to be found in the Old Testament, in passages where God is named *Elohim* (plural of El), with the accompanying verb in the singular. We have endeavored to prove that the use, in Scripture, of this form of expression is one indication, out of many, that the dogma of the Holy Trinity was known and acknowledged among the Ancient Jews.

228. But it is not only in this repeated employment of *Elohim* as a divine Name, that we discover the plural and singular thus curiously associated in the Older Scriptures. We find, in places, the same mode of expression in passages which do not give us the language of the Sacred Chroniclers, but are quotations from the very mouth of God Himself.

229. In Gen. 1:25, 26, 27, we find the following: "And God saw that it was good. And He said: Let *us* make man to our image and likeness. . . . And God created man to his own image; to the image of God he created him; male and female he created them." The intermingling here of the grammatical numbers is repeated and absolutely unmistakable. "And he said" is one singular form and "God created man," etc., is another, and between the two is interposed the plural expression "Let *us* make man" followed by another "to *our* image and likeness."

230. Since these are God's own words, they must have been deliberate; and it cannot be supposed, in this connection, that the Lord did not know, with certainty, all the different interpretations, which were to be suggested from time to time, in explanation of these particular utterances.

231. When, therefore, the Almighty, speaking of Himself, or more properly communing with Himself, thus passes, in these impressive sentences, from singular to plural and then at once back again from plural to singular, there must have been the intent to intimate, in this manner, some great fact, in connection with the divine nature, which in a mysterious way, justly connected with the Almighty the idea of plurality as well as the one of unity.

232. Several methods have been suggested, by Hebrews and others, to account for the peculiar construction of the Scriptural passage last quoted, and others of similar import, so as to avoid conceding that they go to show the existence of the Holy Trinity. One such attempted explanation, generally accepted by the Rabbinical writers, appears in the Jerusalem Targum, as it is now with us,[1] which paraphrases Gen. 1:26 as follows: "Jehova said *to the Angels, ministering before Him, who were created on the second day of the creation of the world.* Let us make man to our image," etc. This rendering has nothing to support it but imagination. Nevertheless, the Rabbis and their followers have presented it as

---

[1] "The Targum text is, taken as a whole, in a very corrupt state." S. M. Schiller-Szinnessy, M. A., Ph. D., in *Encyclopædia Britannica,* Vo. Targum.

the proper one for the passage which is now under consideration: and this, though there is, in this connection, not a word about Angels in the true Genesitic history of Creation, as the same is recorded in the Hebrew Version and in the septuagint.[1] If the Rabbis, in order to uphold their own notions in this regard, must be permitted to thus insert into the true text of Scripture, or to read into the same, whole paragraphs to suit themselves, on the pretext that what is thus interpolated is implied or understood in the original, they must exercise this privilege in opposition to leading canons of literal interpretation, that have been generally adopted, in order that writings may not be left entirely at the mercy of individual caprice.

233.   Indeed, the extract taken as above from the Jerusalem Targum is far from removing the difficulty we are considering.   On the contrary, the only effect it is capable of producing is an additional clouding of the question.   It merely attempts to show that when the Almighty spoke the words recorded in Gen. 1:26 He was addressing the Angels and not self-communing.   But it does not indicate whether the "*us*" includes the Angels with God as actors in the making of man, or whether the Almighty was soliciting the Angelic permission or approval of what He was about to do.   The Targumistic interpolator simply ignored this plain dilemma, though the horns between which it placed him were two rank absurdities.

---

[1] A fact inexplicable, if it be admitted that the Angels were so great and so important as to have been God's Counsellors, in the culminating work of making man.

234. The Talmudists, however, were even less scrupulous, in this regard. With that audacious irreverence which characterized them, at times, even when dealing with the great Jehova, they have plainly pictured the Almighty as seeking the Angelic approval of the divine design, with regard to the making of man; and these actually are the preposterous details, which, on this subject, they have been audacious enough to present: "Rav Jehuda said in the name of Rav; when the Holy One, blessed be He! wished to create a man, He first called into existence a set of ministering Angels, and said to them: 'Is it your pleasure that We should make man in *our* image?' They replied: 'Lord of the Universe! What will be his deeds?' He answered: 'So and so.' They said (Psa. 8:4): 'What is man that thou art mindful of him, and the son of man that thou visitest him?' He then put forth His little finger and destroyed them by fire. A second set shared the same fate. The third set expostulated and said: 'Of what use was it to our predecessors to state their objections? The whole world is Thine, do with it what Thou pleasest.' During the generations, of the deluge and the confusion of tongues, whose deeds were depraved, the Angels said to Him: 'Were not our predecessors right (in objecting to the creation of man)?' God said to them (Isa. 46:4): 'And even to old age I am he, and even to hoar hairs will I carry.' Sanhedrin, fol. 38, col. 2." Hershon, *Genesis, with a Talmudical Commentary*, p. 61.

235. It must be noted that the Talmudists, in excluding, as they do in the passage last quoted, the

angels from active participation in the creation of man, necessarily leave God as, after all, the sole Maker of our human kind, and thus they leave practically untouched the real mystery of verse 26, Chap. 1, of Genesis; which is why the One and Only God should use, in connection *with Himself*, the plurals *"us"* and *"our."* And the imagination of the Rabbis, as above quoted, is not only patently absurd, but it is positively against Holy Scripture, which (Isa. 40:13, 14), puts the following questions: "Who hath forwarded the Spirit of the Lord? or who hath been his Counsellor and hath taught him? With whom hath he consulted? [1] etc."

236.   Dismissing now, as we have the right to do, these extravagant inventions of the Rabbis, and returning to the true text, as found in the Septuagint and in the Hebrew version, we must observe that the only noun appearing anywhere in Genesis and preceding Chap. 1:26, and for which this *"us"* and the *"our"* can be substitutes, is God; and to argue that in this case *"us"* represents not only its expressed antecedent as above, but also the unmentioned angels, and that the *"our"* has also the same relation, is to go contrary to what is plainly written. It is attempting to know better the Sacred Author's thoughts than he knew them himself; it is endeavoring to force him, as it were, to say things which he has abstained from saying.

237.   Though the *"us"* of Gen. 1:26 is in the objective case, in so far as the verb "let" is concerned; yet, in its relation to "make," it is in the

[1] See, also, Wisdom, 9:13; I Cor. 2:13; Rom. 11:34.

nature, as it were, of a subject, inasmuch as it indicates who are about to act as described. If then we are to bring in the angels, so as to cover them also by the term under consideration, we must class the latter as actors in the work indicated by the verb "make," and thus we constitute them Creators with God, and sharers, therefore, of the Divine power. So with the *"our."* If Angels, as well as God, are included within its scope, then are we men made to a double image and likeness, the Divine and the Angelic.

238. Some critics maintain that, in this Scriptural passage, and others of similar construction, God speaks of or rather to Himself, in the manner that He does, as a token of majesty, in the same way as earthly potentates usually do; and such a use of the plural form they name the plural of Majesty.

239. This plural of Majesty is near akin to the plural of excellence that has been suggested in attempted explanation of the use in Gen. 1:1 and elsewhere in Holy Scripture, of the plural form *Elohim,* as a divine name, coupled with a verb in the singular. Both of these above named verbal formations have the same purpose, that of elevating, in the general estimation, the person or thing it is applied to. But, however effective they may prove to such end, whenever the subject is a finite person or thing, they must fail absolutely in their purpose, when there is question of the Omnipotent God, who is infinitely superior to all that He has made, and, therefore, beyond the possibility of being dignified by being compared to any of His creatures, taken either separately or in aggregate.

240.   All, therefore, that we have written in a preceding paper, against the idea that the Scriptural Writers, in employing *Elohim*, with a singular verb, were simply using the Semitic plural, or the plural of excellency, in connection with the Creator of the Universe, applies here again with full force.   Indeed these same objections may be regarded as having stronger force here, for, in Gen. 1:1, and similar passages, God is being spoken of, while in Gen. 1:26, and others of like character, it is the All-Wise God, Himself, who is speaking.

241.   Here another thought suggests itself entirely adverse to all theories, reducing to mere rhetorical forms the intermixtures of singular and plural, to be found in the Sacred Scripture, in connection with the Almighty.   If to pluralize the divine name, or to refer to the Omnipotent God with pronouns in plural form, was calculated to uplift or dignify the Eternal One in any way, how happens it that these expedients were not invariably resorted to throughout the Old Testament, wherever it was possible, instead of using them only rarely as the Sacred Writers have done?   Within the brief compass of the very passage with which we have been particularly dealing, Gen. 1:25, 26, 27, the Almighty is referred to, by name or pronominally, ten times; and out of these ten references two only are in plural form.

242.   Furthermore, though in verse 27 of Genesis 1, God does refer to Himself twice plurally, "*Let* us make Man to *our* image and likeness," nevertheless He returns immediately thereafter to the singular, saying, verse 29, "Behold *I* have given you every

herb, etc." If, therefore, the Lord considered it expedient to apply to Himself twice, in Gen. 1:26, plural pronouns, for the purpose merely of impressing the world with a sense of the amplitude of His divine Majesty, it seems strange that He should have permitted the Inspired Writers to refer to Him, in this one same passage, so repeatedly in the singular. And stranger still is it that He should seemingly have forgotten so soon this particular purpose, and, in the second verse succeeding 29, returned to the singular in speaking of Himself: "Behold *I* have given you, etc."

243. The theory that the plurals here are used to indicate the way in which God summons Himself to energy is hazy and fantastic. If God be All-Powerful, no act of creation can be difficult to Him in the slightest degree. A simple act of His will must be sufficient to produce any result, however stupendous. What, therefore, has He to do with "energy" in any proper acceptation of the term? What intelligible thought is conveyed, when the Omnipotent is spoken of as summoning Himself to work? And, after all, what shadow of justification is there for the notion that, because merely the Almighty occasionally speaks of Himself plurally, He intended thereby to suggest in any way the idea of a self-summoning of any sort?

244. Somewhat akin to the interpretation last dealt with and even more unphilosophical, if possible, is that of Dillman, who is of opinion that God, engaged in the crowning work of making man, addresses Himself in the plural as the complex of all

the divine energies and powers. Complex is an impossible term to use in connection with God. A complex is a definite whole, made up of a variety of finite parts or elements. But no accumulation of mere finites can possibly make up an infinite; therefore, since God is Infinitude itself, He cannot be considered as a Complex.

245. If, however, we are disposed to pass over this initial difficulty in Dillman's hypothesis; this hypothesis seems to imply that God is constituted of "energies and powers," and that, in the making of man, all these "energies and powers" were called into play, while, as to the rest of creation such was not the case. If so, were not all things outside of man created by a part only of God; He being a mere combination of "energies and powers," and His entire "Complex" having been put to work only when man was made?

246. If the act of creation is not to be considered, in any of its phases, as involving any effort on the part of the Almighty God; if the making of man could draw no more heavily upon the divine Omnipotence than could the summoning into existence of one single atom of matter out of nothing, how can it be imagined that the Lord, in Gen. 1 :26, or elsewhere, by addressing Himself plurally, is commemorating a difference, impossible to be conceived, between the exercise on one occasion rather than upon another, of the "divine energies and powers"?

247. But, whatever semblance of justification some may think they find for any of the theories that have been advanced for the purpose of explaining,

from an anti-Trinitarian standpoint, the unusual grammatical construction in Gen. 1 :26, the same cannot reasonably be applied, when it comes to dealing with other passages showing similar formations, to be found in the Old Testament. Some of these are as follows:

1. In the story of the first sin in the Garden it is written: "And He (God) said: Behold Adam is become as one of *Us*." Gen. 3 :22.

2. In the account of the building of the Tower of Babel, and the Confusion of Tongues: "Behold it is one people . . . come *ye*, therefore, let *us* confound their tongues." Gen. 11 :6, 7.

3. "And I heard the voice of the Lord saying: Whom shall *I* send? Who shall go for *us?* And I said: Lo, here am I; send me." Isa. 6 :8.

248. With regard to the passage last quoted, the proposition that the *"us"* found therein is a plural, used for the purpose of including not only God, but also the Seraphim, mentioned in other verses of the same chapter, is untenable. Such an interpretation implies that the demands of the Lord, recorded as above, were addressed primarily to the Seraphim, which was evidently not the case. The divine words were intended for Isaiah, as the text plainly shows. "I heard," the Inspired Writer declares, "the voice of the Lord, saying," etc. "And the Prophet it was who replied at once: 'Lo, here am I: send me.' " And this was immediately after one of the Seraphim had specially fitted Isaiah for the task he was about to undertake, by touching his lips with a coal of fire and cleansing him from sin.

249.   But it would not clear the difficulty, or explain the reason for this use here of the "I" and the "us" in the passage we are considering merely to show that the Lord was addressing the Seraphim, and not Isaiah in the call recorded here.   The personal pronouns in question stand in this place for the questioner and not for the questioned.   To include the Seraphim with Jehova, as uttering the "Who shall go for us?" is to attempt associating creature with the Creator, in a manner irreverent and absurd, and upon terms approaching equality.

250.   It will be observed that the same question, with a slight variation in form, is propounded twice successively in Isa. 6:8: "Whom shall *I* send: Who shall go for *us?*"   Each expression is a thought of the All-Wise God.   There must, therefore, be absolute consonance between them, which cannot be, if the pronouns "I" and "we" therein are to be interpreted as referring to different antecedents.   But, if "I" and "we," as here used, are true equivalents, standing for the same antecedent, God, the meaning must be that the Almighty is of such a nature that He may be rightly spoken of in both singular and plural terms, which can only logically be under the dogma of the Trinity: God One, but in Three Divine Persons.

251.   There are other passages, in the Old Testament, which may be regarded as more or less in line with those quoted above, but a brief mention of them is all that our purpose requires here.   In Dan. 4:14 (17), "the Watchers" and "the Holy Ones" are mentioned almost in the same breath with "the Most

High": and in Dan. 7:9, it is said, "I beheld 'til *thrones were set* and the Ancient of Days sat."

252. We have heretofore called attention to the discussion which prevailed between the early Christians of Jewish blood, and their unconverted Brethren, over the true import of these striking passages, and others of like nature, that are found in the Old Testament. The following, from the Talmud, furnishes an interesting summary, as it were, from the Rabbinical standpoint, of these discussions; and it serves to show how hard put were the Rabbis, in their efforts to meet these attacks of their Christian neighbors. The translation which we present is from Hershon's *Genesis, with a Talmudic Commentary*, pp. 61, 62:

"II. Rabbi Yochanan also said: 'Wherever the *Sadducees'* [1] showed their recklessness, there also their refutation is found. If it be said (Gen. 1:26, 27): 'Let *us* make man to *our* image,' it is added 'God created (singular) man in his image.' 'Let us go down and let *us* confound their languages'; 'And the Lord came down (singular) to see the city and tower.' (Gen. 11:5, 7.) 'For there the Gods (*Elohim*) appeared unto him'; 'Who answered (singular) me in the day of my distress.' (Gen. 35:3, 7.) 'For what nation is there so great who has the gods (*Elohim*) so nigh as Jehova our *God* in all things that we call upon Him for.' (Deut. 4:7.) 'And what one nation in the earth is like thy people like Israel, whom the *Gods* (Elohim) *went* to redeem as a people to *himself*.'

[1] This term *Sadducees* here used means Christians.

(2 Sam. 7:23.) 'The *thrones* were set and the *Ancient* (singular) of days did sit.' (Dan. 7:9.)

"III.   But why use the plural at all (asks some one)?   That is, according to Rabbi Yochanan, who said: The Holy One, blessed be He! never does anything without consulting the Supernal family: as it is said (Dan. 4:14, A. V. 17): 'This matter is by the decree of the *Watchers,* and the demand by the word of the Holy Ones.'

"IV.   But all the rest may be right, and yet why should there be required more than one throne?   It may be said: One for Himself, and One for David; for it is taught by Post-Mischnic tradition: One for Himself and One for David; such are the words of Rabbi Akiva.   But Rabbi Yosi said: 'Akiva! how long wilt thou render the Sheckinah profane,' etc."

253.   We have already called attention to the fact that the problem to be solved in all these passages is not so much why the plural should be used at all, as above suggested, as why the plural and singular, both should be so closely intermixed, in speaking of God.   It is no answer to this difficulty to say that the singular terms correct the plural ones: for, we may ask, in that view, why should confusion be so often uselessly created, and why should the same contradiction be so frequently reproduced in the Sacred Text?   If, indeed, it be that these plural forms need correction, it must be because their repeated use in this connection constitutes a grave mistake, often repeated and stubbornly adhered to.

254.   We have seen, in the first portion of this

chapter, how, in a desperate attempt to explain these peculiar grammatical constructions, Rabbi Yehudah said in the name of Rav," that the *"us"* and the *"our,"* of Gen. 1 :26, were used by the Almighty in addressing three successive crops of angels: while, as appears in our last quotation, Rabbi Yochanan pretends that these two plurals, with all others of similar sort in Holy Scripture, take in "the Supernal family." And Akiva, struggling with the same difficulty, as presented by Dan. 4:14 (17), is driven to placing David upon a superior throne, like unto God Himself.

255. The only reasonable solution of our entire problem lies in the fact that the various passages of Holy Writ, upon which we have been commenting, recognize and rest upon the fact that the nature of God is such as to render the singular and plural properly interchangeable, where used in reference to Him, and this, for the reason that, though there be but One Almighty, that One Almighty is composed of three Divine Persons.

CHAPTER VIII.

Is Man to the Image of the Trinity?

256. WE HAVE heretofore considered the frequent employment of alternating singular and plural forms in the Old Testament, closely associated and used in connection with God; and from this we have reasoned that the mystery of the Holy Trinity was known among the Ancient Hebrews. In our last chapter we dealt, among other things, with this peculiarity of grammatical construction, as it is to be found in the Scriptural account of the creation of man, quoting and discussing at some length the words of the paragraph (Gen. 1:26, 27), "Let *us* make man to *our* image and likeness," etc. It is now in order for us to study more closely the manner in which man has been made to resemble his Creator, and to ascertain whether there is anything in the human constitution that reflects, as it were, the great mystery of the Trinity.[1]

257. If the triple Personage of God be conceded, it is reasonable to look for some showing, or manifestation, of this divine characteristic in man, who

[1] The fact is significant that God, in such immediate connection with the announcement of His intention to create man, passes over, as though abruptly, to the plural form in designating Himself: "Let us make man to our image and likeness." It serves to support the theory advocated in the text of this chapter, that man was made in some special manner, to the image of the Holy Trinity; or, as Holy Scripture expresses it, in God's own words, "to *our* image and likeness."

has been made, as we know, to the divine image. Indeed, by some it may be considered necessary, in order to vindicate the dogma of the Holy Trinity, to show that man has something of the triune in his nature, and resembles, therefore, in this essential respect, his divine Prototype, Who is in Heaven.[1]

258. For our present purposes we may consider man in two aspects, generically and individually: and if from either of these points of view a resemblance between him and the Holy Trinity be discovered, our position is established. Indeed, the manner in which the history of man's creation is related in Genesis justifies the conclusion that the Sacred Writer intended to present this great event to us under the two aspects above suggested.

259. For the convenience of our readers, we now reproduce, from the First Book of Holy Scripture, the several references to the creation of man, in it contained as follows:

"And he said, let us make man to our image and likeness; and let *him* have dominion over the fishes of the sea, and the fowls of the air, and the beasts and the whole earth, and every creeping creature

[1] We do not wish to be understood as holding that all the interpretations contended for in this chapter are essential. God might have created man to His image, so far alone as He Himself is One; and the absence in our human constitution of anything particularly suggestive of the Holy Trinity would not have falsified Sacred Scripture in this regard, and left man unlike his Maker, in respect to freedom, wisdom and immortality. But, even our natural reason seems to suggest the probability that a divine characteristic so distinguishing as the Holy Trinity should find a manifestation of some sort in man, and seems to justify the reflex argument that if man, the image, be shown to be in any way triune, God, the Model, may be judged to be the same.

that moveth upon the earth. And God created man to his own image: to the image of God he created *him: male and female he created them.*" Gen. 1:26, 27.

"And the Lord God formed man out of the slime of the earth: and breathed into his face the breath of life, and man became a living soul. And the Lord God had planted a paradise of pleasure from the beginning; wherein he placed man, whom he had formed." Gen. 2:7, 8.

"And Adam called all the beasts by their names, and all the fowls of the air, and all the cattle of the field; but for Adam there was not found a helper like himself. And the Lord God cast a deep sleep upon Adam, and when he was fast asleep, he took one of his ribs, and filled up flesh for it. And the Lord God built the rib which he took from Adam into a woman, and brought her to Adam. And Adam said: This now is bone of my bones, and flesh of my flesh; she shall be called Woman, *because she was taken out of man.* Wherefore a man shall leave father and mother, and shall cleave to his wife: and they shall be *two in one flesh.*" Gen. 2:20 to 24.

"This is the book of the generation of Adam. In the day that God created *man*, he made *him* to the likeness of God. He created *them* male and female; and blessed them: and called *their name Adam*, in the day when they were created." Gen. 5:1, 2.

260. Some contend that the several extracts given above are mere repetitions, due to the facts that the same, or a similar story, had been told by two or more ancient authors, and that a later com-

piler, seeking to combine all preceding accounts into
one, chose from different older manuscripts the passages above quoted and reproduced them as they
had been originally written. We are not called upon
to discuss at any length the question whether Moses
was or was not the author of Genesis; for, in any
view, the fact remains that the passages with which
we are dealing form parts of the oldest sacred literature of the Hebrews; and if, as such, they furnish
any support for the proposition that the dogma of
the Holy Trinity was known and acknowledged in
oldest Judaism, our immediate purpose is fully met.

261. We may remark, however, that, even if it be
conceded that the quotations given above from the
second and fifth chapters of Genesis are mere repetitions, this fact would furnish no sound argument
in favor of the theory that Moses did not write, or
cause to be written, or compile, or cause to be com-
piled, the entire Book of Genesis. The theory of the
verbal inspiration of Holy Writ is not compulsory
upon Christian believers, particularly so as to its
text as we now have it, after having suffered the
mutations of thousands of years. We might, therefore, safely concede that Moses was faulty in his
own rhetoric, or that he adopted the faulty rhetoric
of others, provided only that we insist upon the absolute truth, throughout, of the message, such as he
has given it. If Moses loved repetitions, he has had
many imitators; and, indeed, repetition, for the purpose of clearness or emphasis, is often inevitable.

262. Even if some of the passages quoted above
be repetitions, in a strict sense, the importance of

the event recorded was in itself warrant enough to Moses for bringing it repeatedly, and in different forms of expression, to the attention of his people, so that they might fully apprehend and faithfully remember the great truth, that man alone, among all visible creatures, has been made to the image and likeness of God.

263.   Furthermore, Gen. 1:26, 27, first quoted above, is a part of the general narrative of all creation, a verbal panorama of the great work in its entirety: and it tells, consequently, of the creation of man as the culminating one of a series of divine acts.   Gen. 2:7, 8, also quoted above, takes up, in particular, the early history of humanity and very properly introduces this subject by referring again to the fact that man was made by God, adding the details, not before mentioned, that Adam was made out of the slime of the earth, and that a soul was breathed into him by the Almighty.

264.   Gen. 2:20, *et seq.*, is a continuation of this primitive history of the human race, affording important additional information, as it tells how woman was brought into being, after Adam's formation, and that in the act the divine purpose was that she might be to him "a helper like himself."

265.   The fifth chapter of Genesis is, as its opening words declare, the "book of the Generation of Adam," and its verses detail the genealogy, the names, ages, deaths, etc., of a long line of Patriarchs, who were from Adam, down to Noe and his sons.   It is submitted, in this connection, that the majority of men, called upon to write a paper or chapter de-

voted to the line or descent of some great historical family, would preface their work, as in this instance, by a few words, recalling the root or origin whence came the original father of that particular race or stock.

266. It is further contended that, not only are the different scriptural accounts, or references, above quoted, faulty repetitions, but they are also contradictory. It is pretended that Gen. 1:26, 27, details the making of man and woman, at one and the same time and in the same way, whereas Gen. 2:7 and 2:20, *et seq.*, announce that Adam was made first, out of the slime of the earth, and that Eve, later, was taken from the side of the man.

267. Gen. 1:26, 27, does not declare that Adam and Eve were created both at the same time and in the same manner. It says simply: "And God created man to his own image: to the image of God He created him: male and female he created them." Nothing is here set forth that excludes the idea that Adam was created at one time and in one way and Eve shortly afterward and in another way. And, if the same historian, who tells us in a general fashion, in his first chapter, of the making of man, male and female, enters later into more details, and states the time and manner of the making of the first representative of each sex, upon what principle are the two recitals to be judged as conflicting?

268. When Gen. 1:27 says, in a general way, "male and female he created them," we may consider that this statement summarizes in a few words the entire work, and that the distinction of sex was

established only when Eve was taken from the side
of Adam. Or, we may hold that man, generally considered, was created in and represented by Adam,
from whom Eve herself was shortly to come, and
that, when in Adam the human race was thus made
and established, it was endowed with a nature essentially bi-sexual. In this last view, Adam would
stand, at least during the earlier hours of his existence, not only for himself, but for Eve also, who, by
divine operation, was soon to spring from his side,
and for all of the innumerable progeny which in the
process of time was to descend from him.[1] This
latter theory has apparently the support of Gen.
5:1, 2: "In the day that God created *man*, he created *him* to the likeness of God. He created *them*
male and female: and blessed *them* and called *their*
name Adam, in the day when *they were created*."

269. To the same effect, in this regard, seems
Gen. 1:26, 27, when critically considered: "And he
said, let us make *man* to our image and likeness, let

[1] Gen. 1:28, 29, adds in no way to the difficulty. "And
God blessed them, saying: Increase and multiply. . . . And
behold I have given you every herb," etc. These words may
have been spoken only after Adam and Eve were both in
being, as recited in Gen. 2:7 and 21, *et seq.;* or, at the outset, God may have blessed the race in its entirety, and given
to it the commission to rule—all in Adam, who was the father
of all. Certain it is that we of this day still increase and
multiply, and we rule over and make use of the beasts and
the plants. Concede these to be two primitive blessings, as Holy
Scripture recites, and it must be granted that we, who are now
living, received them, not each personally, but all of us through
Adam, our first Father. And if, for the purpose of receiving
these divine blessings, we of this time can be considered as
having been present at the beginning, in Adam, why not Eve,
also, who was as much as ourselves an offspring from the
original human father?

him have dominion. . . . And God created *man* to his own image and likeness; to the image of God he created *him:* male and female he created *them.*"

270. Let us observe the indiscriminate use in these passages of *him* and *them,* an indiscrimination that seems unintelligible, unless it be from the point of view that, prior at least to the appearance of Eve, Adam stood for himself and his race, created in him and all to come from him, the first woman included. If this be not so, it might be urged that Eve was not made to the image of God, for it is said: "And God created *man* to his own image: to the image of God he created *him.*" Indeed, with regard to Eve, it may be maintained that she was to be the divine image because she was made like Adam: "And the Lord said: It is not good for man to be alone: let us make him a help *like unto himself.*" Gen. 2:18.

271. Adam, when created, was given a soul,[1] with three powers: will, memory and understanding. These three powers have a distinctiveness which we all must recognize; and yet they are so essentially united and interdependent as to form a unit and to constitute together but one spirit.[2] It is true that

[1] We may refer in passing to the fact that in man's constitution or nature alone it is, that the three great divisions or kingdoms of created things are represented. The matter of his body unites him with the mineral; the physical life that is in him incorporates him into the kingdom of visible living things; and his immortal soul shows him part of the highest division of all, the truly spiritual. This triple composition of the human beings is not unsuggestive of the Holy Trinity, but we do not dwell upon it, for there are other respects in which the resemblance is more patent and more impressive.

[2] We are not oblivious of the fact that many deny the very existence of the human soul, and, by consequence, deny its

many and wide differences may be suggested between the soul of man, with its three powers, and the Triune God. So it must be, for the latter is infinite, the former finite only. Holy Scripture does not say that man, when created, became God, or that he was made the same as God: it declares only that he was made to the divine image. The portrait upon the wall, the statue upon its base may be excellent likenesses of their originals; but, after all, one is only canvas and paint and the other bronze or marble. The lower animals may be said to be, in a way, the images of man; but, despite certain structural and other resemblances, how vast the difference that remains.

272. But it is, perhaps, in the general constitution of human nature that we find the clearest reminder of the Holy Trinity. Humanity's unit is not so much the individual as it is the family: father, mother and child. These three, though distinct, if considered individually, are yet necessary adjuncts, one of the other, brought together in a combination, ordained by God, for the purpose of establishing the home and perpetuating our kind.

273. The dogma of the Holy Trinity, as most generally accepted among Christians, is that God the

three powers. The arguments set forth in this paper can be of little avail, probably, with such. Fortunately, however, the great majority of enlightened men prefer to accept what appears to them the evidence of their own consciousness and experience in this regard, rather than the argumentations of Physicists, who seek to persuade us all that there is no power within us which considers and judges; none which remembers and forgets; none which, by the exercise within of its fiat or its veto, controls our conduct and regulates, or at least affects, our relations with the external world.

Son is the Only Begotten of God the Father, from eternity, and that God, the Holy Ghost, proceeded, eternally also, from both the Father and the Son. We find this same order observed in the creation of the human family, as related in Holy Writ: Eve was from the side of Adam, and was bone of his bone and flesh of his flesh, and from both Adam and Eve came the child.[1] True, in the constitution of the human family, we have a dim figure only of the Holy Trinity, throwing a little light upon the impenetrable mystery of the divine Triune nature; but showing practically nothing of how it is that the Heavenly Father begot the Eternal Son, and how, from these two Eternal Persons proceeded the equally Eternal Holy Ghost.[2]

[1] "And Adam knew Eve, his wife, who conceived and brought forth Cain, saying I have gotten a man through God." Gen. 4:1.

[2] The mystery of the Holy Trinity is not contrary to our finite human reason; it is beyond it. The same is to be said of mysteries which confront us in the order of material creation. Do we understand anything of the true nature and extent of space; anything ultimately of being, matter force or life? The question of the Holy Trinity is not at all one of possibility or impossibility, for we are here dealing with the Omnipotent God, and there are for Him no impossibilities. The proposition for us here is simply whether or not this dogma has been revealed by God Himself. If we believe that God has revealed it, we may accept it without violence to our reason, for we must recognize that these things are upon a plane that is higher than that of our human comprehension. As to the eternity of the begetting of God, the Son, and the eternity likewise of the procession of God the Holy Ghost from Father and Son, this is not in itself a difficulty, because, if we concede the facts themselves, it is impossible to conceive a period anywhere in the eternity of the past, when this begetting of the Son and this procession of the Holy Ghost were impossibilities. It is here somewhat the same as with matter: it seems hard to think of it as eternally created; but, granted

274. With the deeper problems, suggested by our subject, we are not concerned in this article, which has for its purpose merely to show that the Old Testament, read in connection with certain physical and psychological facts, shows that man has been made to the image and likeness of the Holy Trinity.   The Almighty might have created man otherwise than with one soul, possessed of three constitutive powers, and He might have provided some other way, or means, than the family, father, mother and child, for increasing and multiplying the human race.   But He has not done otherwise, in either regard, and we are free to maintain that, what He has done, in both cases, has been done in order that man might disclose, in a double manner and more clearly, that he has been made in the likeness of the Triune God.

275. It is no answer to this contention to suggest that animals, also, possess will, memory and understanding and that some of them increase in the same way as man does. It is no easy task to determine to what extent the actions of animals are instinctive merely and not truly mental. Be this as it may, the internal impulses, or powers if we choose to style them such, that direct the actions and shape

an Omnipotent and Eternal God, can we conceive of one single moment during the eternal past, when the creation of matter was an impossibility to the Lord? As for the objection that our dogma suggests changes in the changeless nature of God, we know only in the dimmest way our own nature, and the natures of the visible things which are about us. What, therefore, can we know of the ultimate nature of God, and why should any undertake to pronounce with such assurance upon what must be and what must not be a change in that fundamental divine nature?

the lives of the brutes, constitute collectively and at their best, a mere likeness, extremely faint, of the human soul. And the Almighty may well be considered as having created the animals to the likeness of man, just as man himself has been made to the image and likeness of God. The fact that animals were brought into actual physical being before man has no bearing upon the question. With God there is an eternal present.[1] Before even the lowest living form was placed upon the earth, indeed from all Eternity itself, the entire plan of living creation was present, all complete, in the mind of God.

[1] "And Jesus said to them: Amen, Amen, I say to you, before Abraham was made, I am." John 8:58.

CHAPTER IX.

"In the Vale of Mambre."—Genesis 18.

276. The eighteenth chapter of Genesis, in connection with the nineteenth, presents to the thoughtful student several difficulties. To some extent these may be occasioned by interpolations, or by variations of other kinds, from an original text; but, in large measure, they are due also to a persistent refusal, on the part of many, to recognize the fact that this eighteenth chapter has reference to the three divine Persons, composing the HOLY TRINITY.

277. There are, in the account of Abraham's vision in the Vale of Mambre, the same intermingling of singular and plural, while speaking of God, and rapid transitions from one form to the other, similar to those so often to be found in other parts of the Old Testament, and which go to prove that, from remote antiquity, the mystery of the Holy Trinity was known among the Jews.

278. The following is a skeleton extract from the eighteenth chapter of Genesis, in which words showing the changes in number already referred to are in italics:

"And *the Lord* (Jehova) appeared to him. . . . There appeared to him *three* men. . . . And as soon as he saw *them* he ran to meet *them*. . . . And he said *Lord*, if I have found favor in *thy* sight, pass not away from *thy* servant: but I will fetch a

little water and wash *ye your* feet and rest *ye* under
the tree. . . . Strengthen *ye* your heart, after-
wards *you* shall pass on: for therefore are *you* come
aside to *your* servant, and *they* said: Do as thou
hast spoken. . . . And when *they* had eaten, *they*
said to him: Where is Sara, thy wife? He answered
lo, she is in the tent: and *he* said to him, *I*
will return. . . . And the *Lord* said to Abraham . . . is there anything hard to *God?*
According to appointment *I* will return. . . . And
the men rose up from there. . . . And Abraham
walked with *them.* . . . And *the Lord* said, can *I*
hide from Abraham what *I* am about to do. . . .
For *I* know he will command his children. . . .
And the *Lord* said *I* will go down and see. . . .
And *they* turned *themselves* from thence and went
their way to Sodom: But Abraham yet stood before
the Lord," etc.

279. That this chapter is intended to record the
appearance of God, Himself, to Abraham seems
clear. In the first place, the word in the opening
verse, rendered usually into English by "Lord," is in
the original "Jehova," a name that was reserved
among the olden Jews exclusively for the one and
only true God. Again, in the original text we find,
verse 13, *"Jehova* said to Abraham," etc.; and in
verse 14, "is there anything hard to *Jehova";* and in
verse 22, "Abraham stood before *Jehova."*

280. A careful study of the first and second
verses of this same chapter must lead us to this same
conclusion: for, in the first verse, it is declared that
Jehova appeared to Abraham, as the latter was "sit-

ting in the door of his tent, in the very heat of the day," and the second follows immediately, without a break or interruption of any sort, telling how, when the Patriarch "had lifted up his eyes, there appeared to him *three men,* standing near him." If the "*three men*" that Abraham saw, when he lifted up his eyes, and whom he ran to meet, and whom he "adored down to the ground," whom he entertained so lavishly, were not Jehova, then what became of Jehova, after He had made his appearance, as related in the opening words of the chapter? What occasion was there for the appearance of the "*three men*" simultaneously with Jehova; and how is it that Abraham turned his back upon his God, running to meet the men and "adoring" them "down to the ground"?

281. In their hostility to Christianity and its cardinal dogma, the Divinity of Christ, some of the Rabbinical writers have gone to the extent of suggesting, in face of the clear showing of Genesis to the contrary, that the three men who appeared to Abraham in the Vale of Mambre were angels. Nevertheless some of these writers have, at the same time taught that the first verse of this chapter refers to Jehova, Himself.

282. In the Talmud (Bava-Metzia, fol. 86, col. 2) is the following:

"Rav Channa bar Chanena said: That day was the third after Abraham's circumcision [1] (Gen. 34, 25);

---

[1] To understand fully this extract and some others, from the Talmud, reference must be had to Chap. 17 of Genesis, which tells of the circumcision of Abraham and his household. The third day after the performance of this rite is generally one of most suffering and is marked usually with some fever. Gen. 34:25.

therefore, the Holy One, blessed be He! came to visit him, and at the same time, He divested the sun of its cover (*Narthik*), that he might not be molested by wayfarers. But Abraham sent Eliezer to look out for them, and when he could find none, Abraham would not believe him. Hence they say in Palestine: Servants cannot be trusted. Just when Abraham was on the point of going to look out for himself, the Holy One, blessed be He! presented Himself at the door." [1]

283. In the Treatise *Sota*, fol. 14, *recto*, it is said:

"R. Hhama-bar-Hahnina says: What is the meaning of this verse: Follow the Lord, your God, Deut. 13:5? How can a man march behind the Divinity, since it is written, *Because the Lord thy God is a consuming fire*, Deut. 4:24? But he means imitate the works of charity of the Most Holy, blessed be He! Clothe the poor, who are naked, as He gave covering to the nudity of Adam and Eve; visit the sick, as He visited Abraham in his illness."

284. The Zohar has, in this connection, part, MYSTERIES OF THE LAW, the following:

"*And Jehova appeared to him;* manifestation of the divine essence under the three principal colors, as it is above in the heaven. And it is in the same number of colors that God manifests Himself in the rainbow."

The paraphrase [2] of Jonathan-ben-Huziel:

---

[1] See *Genesis, with Talmudical Commentary,* Paul Isaac Hershon, p. 304.

[2] Or Targum.

"And the glory of Jehova revealed itself to him (Abraham) in the plain of Mambre."

The Jerusalem paraphrase:

"And the glory of God revealed itself to him in the plain of the vision." [1]

285. It is maintained by some that verse 22 is opposed to the Trinitarian interpretation of the eighteenth chapter of Genesis, the said verse reading thus: "And they turned themselves from thence and went their way to Sodom, and Abraham yet stood before the Lord." It is argued that the "they" used in said verse 22 stands for two angels, who departed for Sodom, while the third, who was God, remained with Abraham, since the latter, as we are told *"stood before the Lord."*

286. It has been shown that the first part of this chapter indicates that it was Jehova, who appeared in the Vale of Mambre, under the guise of three men; and if the remainder of the chapter gives this meaning unmistakably, verse 22 must be construed, if possible, so as to harmonize with the others, rather than so as to antagonize them.

287. It is true that in Gen. 18:22 it is said that "Abraham as yet *stood before* the Lord"; and if by *"stood before"* we are compelled to understand that the Lord and Abraham came to an actual halt, it may be inferred that the original party of three was here broken up, and two only went on toward Sodom. But the *"stood before"* here employed does not refer to any mere physical action upon the part of Abra-

[1] See Drach, *De l'Harmonie entre l'Eglise et la Synagogue,* Vol. I, p. 450.

ham, but describes the intellectual one of pleading for the fated city. All lexicographers give, as synonymous to the verb to stand, in one of its senses, the other verbs to withstand, to resist, to oppose. The earnest and persistent plea which the Patriarch put forth for the inhabitants of Sodom, and which was manifestly in the mind of the inspired writer when he here used the words "yet stood before the Lord," is fully set forth in verses 23 to 33; and there was nothing which rendered it necessary that Abraham and his Divine Lord should be at a standstill, while the former was thus pleading the cause of Sodom.

288. That the *Three* were not separated, and were not intending to separate, when Abraham began his supplication, appears from verses 20, 21 and 22, which are absolutely connected and which declare that: "The Lord said: The cry of Sodom and Gomorrah is multiplied. . . . *I will go down* and see whether they have done according to the cry which has come to *me.* . . . And *they* turned *themselves from thence,* and went *their way to Sodom;* but Abraham as yet stood before the Lord." Here the "I" and the "they" can have but one and the same reference: for the "I will go down," etc., expresses a purpose, the execution of which is shown by the "they" turned "themselves" from thence and went "their" way to Sodom.

289. If one only of the *Three* was Jehova and two were angels, it is strange that they should have appeared all together and *in the same guise* and that there should be no mention, in this circum-

stantial account, of any distinction between them in nature and dignity. Strange that Abraham treated them all alike; [1] that his very first words to them were addressed to all of them conjointly as one being only, "Lord if I have found favor in *thy* sight, pass not away from *thy* servant," while the words immediately following, with unbroken connection, indicate the plurality of persons: ". . . Wash *ye your* feet and rest *ye* under the tree," etc.

290. Returning to verse 22; before conceding that it conflicts with other passages we must weigh its every word carefully. What is the meaning or province of the "yet" which is found here? The Century Dictionary gives it the following definition, "still, in continuance of a former state; at this or that time as formerly; now as then; as at a previous time."

291. Now in verse 21 we are told that the three ("they") "went their way to Sodom," etc. In verse 16 it had been expressly announced that the three "turned their eyes toward Sodom," and that "Abraham *walked with them, bringing them on their way.*" As a rule, events are historically recorded in the order of their occurrence; therefore, what is told in verses 16, 21 and the first part of 22 may be presumed to have preceded in time the event which is related in the concluding words of verse 22. Consequently, it may be considered that, when Abraham

---

[1] It cannot be answered here that Abraham treated all of the three alike, because he did not know the difference, for the theory we are now combatting implies that he marked out Jehova, for he "stood before the Lord." And see verses 13, 15, 17, 20, etc.

began to "stand before the Lord" in behalf of the wicked city, all present were proceeding toward Sodom, and that this was the "former state," which the "yet" of verse 22 was intended to show as still continuing, while Abraham was supplicating the Lord.

292. We have also, in this same paragraph, the conjunction but; "But Abraham yet stood," etc. This particular conjunction is often used in the sense of "however, yet, still, nevertheless, notwithstanding." And the construction of the clause in question, which the use of this "but" justifies, is that, notwithstanding the fact that the *three* had turned *themselves* from thence and *went their way* to Sodom, for the purpose of judging it, Abraham, as a suppliant, began to oppose the design of God.[1]

293. Opponents of the Trinitarian interpretation of Genesis, Chap. 18, place great reliance upon what is written in Chap. 19, which in the Douay translation opens as follows: "And the two Angels came to Sodom in the evening," etc. At first sight, this passage may seem to strongly fortify the inferences that verse 22, Chap. 18, records the actual breaking up of the party of *Three,* who had appeared to Abraham, and that one only of the Three was Jehova, the other two being angels. And verse 13 of this same Chap. 19 is quoted as further strengthening this position: "For we will destroy this place,

[1] The fact of Abraham's "drawing nigh" to God, when he began his pleadings, verse 23, militates somewhat against the idea that it was meant to announce by the words "stood before God," that the Lord and Abraham came at this time to a physical standstill.

because their cry is grown loud before the Lord, *who has sent us to destroy them.*"

294.   This apparent contradiction between the verses referred to in Chap. 19, and certain plain passages, already commented upon, from Chap. 18, is occasioned, in large measure, by the presence, in certain versions, of the definite article "the," in verse 1, Chap. 19, of Genesis.   When we read here, "and *the* two angels came to Sodom," etc., we are apt to conclude that "the two Angels" last mentioned must have been two out of the *three men,* who had appeared to Abraham.[1]   But the articles, definite and indefinite, were unknown in the earliest stages of the historical languages,[2] and we may well suppose that they were not used by the original writer of Genesis.[3]

295.   A later insertion of the definite article in this text may have resulted from an impression, on

[1] The opening of verse 1, Chap. 19, of Genesis with "and" has little significance here, for the word is used in Holy Scripture, with utmost frequency, as a mere introductive, and without intent to show particular connection, or close sequence between what has gone before and what comes after.   Indeed, in many instances, the text itself indicates that events, thus seemingly joined together, have been in fact separated by long intervals.   We find an example of this in Gen. 4:3, "and it came to pass, after many days," etc.

[2] "In no language," says Dr. Latham, "in its oldest stage, is there ever a word giving, in its primary sense, the idea of an or the.   As tongues become modern, some word with a similar sense is used to express the relation.   In course of time a change of form takes place, corresponding to the change of meaning."   *International Cyclopædia,* Vo. Article.

[3] The Vulgate reads: "Veneruntque duo Angeli Sodomam, vespere, etc.   True the Latin has no articles, but a similar restriction might have been shown, if desired, by the use of other forms.   The King James, English Version, renders the verse as follows: "And there came two Angels," etc.

the part of translator or copyist, that Gen. 18:22, indicated separation of the original *Three,* by the stopping still of one (Jehova) to listen to the suplications of Abraham, and the going on of the other two toward Sodom. But this verse, Gen. 18:22, can be made, as we have seen, to agree with its companion passages, that demand so positively a Trinitarian construction; and if there be good reason for dropping the article "the" from Gen. 19:1, it should be done, also for harmony's sake.[1]

296. The two angels, of Genesis 19, were merely to execute a divine sentence. "For we will destroy this place, because their cry is grown loud before the Lord, who hath sent us to destroy them," verse 13. On the other hand, the Three, who appeared to Abraham were judges and not executioners: "I will go down and see whether they have done according to the cry that is come to me; or whether it be not so, that I may know." Gen. 18:21. There is nothing in any of the verses studied in the body of this article, that is fatal to the suggested solution that the Lord, *after having given to Abraham his hearing and after finally condemning Sodom, as having not*

---

[1] Saint Augustine entertained the opinion advocated in this chapter, concerning the true meaning of Chap. 18 of Genesis. "Behold," he says, "how, suddenly, the Incorporeal Majesty descends on earth under the corporeal figure of three men. Abraham runs eagerly to meet them, he extends to them his suppliant hands, kisses their knees and says: 'Lord, if I have found grace before thee pass not away from thy servant. Observe Abraham runs to meet three and adores one: unity in three, Trinity in One. . . . Behold how the Celestial Majesty sits at the table of a mortal, accepts a repast and establishes a familiar conversation between God and man." De Tempore, Sermo. LXVIII, No. 2. Also, same, LXX, No. 4.

even ten virtuous men within its walls, sent angels to carry out, during the next or some other succeeding night, the sentence of condemnation.

297.   Sodom could not have been very far from the Vale of Mambre, where the tent of Abraham was pitched when the Three appeared to him; for, getting up *"early in the morning,"* on the day after the destruction of that wicked city, the Patriarch was able to reach the place where, so shortly before, he had "stood before the Lord," and from thence to witness "the *ashes* rise up from the earth as the smoke of a furnace." [1]   Gen. 19:27. Now the *Three* had appeared to Abraham, "in the heat of the day," which might have been at any time, according to modern reckoning, from nine morning to mid-day.[2] It is almost certain that the repast prepared for the *Three* was dinner, which customarily was given between 10 and 11 A. M.,[3] and surely not later than noon.[4] It is evident that the preparations were hur-

---

[1] Indeed, it is not improbable that the city itself was visible in the distance from the door of Abraham's tent; for "when the men rose up from thence, they turned their eyes toward Sodom." This may be fairly held as implying that the city named was actually in sight.

[2] "In more ancient times the day seems to have been divided merely into four general parts, according to the position of the sun in the heavens. Hence, the notices of its earlier or later periods are expressed only in general terms: such as the morning, the heat of the day, mid-day or noon, the cool of the day and the evening." Nevin's *Biblical Antiquities,* p. 172.

[3] Nevin's *Biblical Antiquities,* p. 111.

[4] "And when he (Joseph) had seen them, and Benjamin with them, he commanded the steward of his house, saying: 'Bring in the men into the house, and kill victims and prepare a feast: because they will eat with me at noon.'" Gen. 43:16; see, also, Hasting's *Dictionary of the Bible,* Vol. II, p. 41.

ried. "Abraham made haste into the tent to Sara and said to her: '*Make haste* and temper together three measures of meal,'" etc., verse 6. "He then *ran* to the herd": and the young man to whom he delivered the selected calf "*made haste* and boiled it." Verse 7.

298. All that is related, in Genesis 18, may have taken place within the space of a few hours, possibly not more than three. Therefore, it was probably all at an end by three o'clock, afternoon. And as the destroying Angels did not appear in Sodom until "in the evening," which was any time from six to nine P. M., by present reckoning,[1] there must have been some break of continuity between the events recited in the two chapters we are considering. And, indeed, if we omit, for reasons above given, the first definite article found in some versions of verse 1 of Chap. 19, there is nothing which compels us to hold that the visit of angels to Sodom occurred upon the same day as did the appearance of Jehova, under the guise of "three men," to Abraham.

299. But, suppose, after all, that it be conceded, for the sake of argument, that the passages, from Gen. 18:19, relied upon in this discussion by anti-Trinitarians, cannot be read otherwise than as they themselves interpret them, the only result must be to make this portion of Holy Scripture contradictory. No matter how these particular verses may be con-

[1] "The first watch, or evening, lasted till about nine o'clock of our time: the second, or midnight from nine to twelve: the third, or cock-crowing, from twelve to three; the fourth, or morning, from three till it was day." Nevin's *Biblical Antiquities,* p. 173.

strued, they cannot take away from the plain sense of the numerous other passages, from Chap. 18, which go positively to show that the *"Three men"* of Abraham's vision, in the Vale of Mambre, and the great Jehova were the same. Interpretation, by references to context, may explain what is ambiguous but it cannot be used to destroy what is clear.

300.   Even were it a fact, therefore, that one set of verses here must seem in conflict with another set, this would not take away from the effect of the passages, in Genesis 18, which are corroborative of the other evidences from Holy Scripture in the same general line; all supporting the proposition that the mystery of the Holy Trinity was not unknown among the ancient Jews.

301.   When truth demands it, Catholics need not shrink from granting the existence of occasional conflicts in the text of Holy Writ as that text has come down to us, after having endured the chances of thousands of years. That all which was given originally to the Sacred Writers, under both dispensations, was inspired we firmly hold, and also that we have, with comparatively little alteration, what was originally so written. But we are not compelled to contend that in the course of long centuries there have been no "glosses and explications interpolated into the text," no "words and forms of discourse translated from older into a more modern style," no "faulty readings attributable to the unskillfulness of copyists." And, whenever we encounter such "faulty readings," such "glosses and explications interpolated into the text," etc., we may feel that "it is

lawful to investigate and judge according to the laws of criticism"; this, of course under the condition, "due regard being paid to the judgment of the Church." [1]

[1] See Answers of Biblical Commission to Five Questions, issued July 22, 1906: N. Y. Freeman's *Journal,* August 11, 1906.

CHAPTER X.

"The Angel of Jehova."

302. There are many passages in the Old Testament in which the *Angel of Jehova* is represented as acting with and towards the world and mankind in such ways as to justify the conclusion that this name, like those heretofore considered (the Word of Jehova and Wisdom), applies to one of the divine Persons. If this be so, then all of these three names must be held as variations in the manner of indicating one and the same Divine Being; and all that goes to show the use, for this purpose, of any and all of these designations, must be taken together. Thus cumulated, the numerous passages from Sacred Scripture, referring to *the Word*, to *the Wisdom* and to *the Angel of Jehova* present an irresistible weight of proof in support of the dogma of the Holy Trinity. Furthermore, since these passages relate, all of them, to the same subject matter, they must serve, each and every one, to interpret the others and to enlighten their obscurities.

303. We first meet with this expression: *"The Angel of Jehova,"* in the Old Testament in Chap. 16 of Genesis, where we are told of the birth of Ismael and of events immediately following. There it is related that, after Agar, the mother, had fled from the presence of Sarai, the Angel of the Lord (Jehova) appeared to the bondwoman and bade her return and humble herself to her mistress, telling her at the same time of the future in store for her child and his posterity. Holy Writ here makes of Agar a positive witness, establishing the divinity of the Angel of the Lord. "And she called the name of the Lord that spoke unto her: Thou the God who hast seen me. . . . Therefore she called that well the well of him that liveth and seeth me," etc. Gen. 16:13, 14. The Angel gives also similar testimony: "And again he said: *I* will multiply thy seed exceedingly, and it shall not be numbered for multitude." Gen. 16:10. Here it is the Angel Himself who is to multiply the seed of Ismael. We cannot read this verse as meaning that the Lord, as distinguished from the Angel, was to do this; that the Angel, in other words, was announcing only what was to be performed by another than himself.

304. Later we read in Genesis, Chap. 21, how Agar, with her son Ismael, was sent forth from the home of Abraham; and how the mother, lost in the wilderness, and reduced to despair, abandons her child to death, as she thought. "*God* heard the voice of the boy," says Holy Scripture, "and an *Angel of God* called to Agar from heaven, saying: What art thou doing, Agar? Fear not; for *God* hath heard the voice of the boy. . . . And *God* opened her eyes," etc. Gen. 21:17, 18, 19.

305. The Douay translation has here "an angel," as quoted above; but, in the Vulgate, the article is of course omitted: "Vocavitque Angelus Dei Agar de cœlo." The King James and the Revised Version both give here the definite article: "*the* Angel of God

called to Agar," etc. Recurring to the Vulgate, it
seems evident that the *Deus* and the *Angelus Dei* of
verse 17 are one and the same Being. The passage
deals with one continuous divine action; the hearing
of the infant's distressful cry, and the calling, because thereof, to Agar. Not a word intervenes between the two names to suggest any difference in
their application. There is no mention of any command by God to any Angel, simply such, to speak for
Him on this occasion; and, since there was no visible
appearance of any sort to Agar, no necessity is
shown why "an Angel" should call out to her "from
Heaven," in the place of God Himself. As a rule, he
who hears responds, and for "an Angel" to have answered in this case for God, without command, would
have beeen a gross irreverence.

306. The twenty-second chapter of Genesis re-
counts the circumstances of Abraham's proposed
sacrifice to God of his son, Isaac. Verses 11 and 12
read: "And behold the *Angel of Jehova*, from
heaven, called to him, saying: Abraham, Abraham.
And he answered: Here I am. And he said to him:
Lay not thy hand upon the boy, neither do thou anything to him; now *I* know *that thou fearest God*, and
hast not spared thy only begotten son *for my sake*."

307. And verse 14 adds, "And he called the name
of the place the Lord Seeth (Jehova-Jireh). Whereupon even to this day it is said: In the mountain the
Lord (Jehova) will see."

308. Verse 15, *et seq.*, tells how the Angel of
Jehova called to Abraham a second time from heaven
saying: "*By my own self* have I sworn, said *the Lord*

(Jehova) . . . *I will bless thee, I will multiply thy seed,"* etc.

309. In Genesis, Chap. 31, Jacob relates one of his visions to Rachel and Lia. Among other things he says to them, verse 11: "And the *Angel of God* said to me in my sleep: Jacob? And I answered: Here I am." And this Angel of God who thus called to Jacob makes the following plain statement of His own Divinity, verse 13: "*I am the God of Bethel,* where thou didst anoint the stone and made a vow to me."

310. This reference in Gen. 31:13 can only be to that other vision vouchsafed to Jacob and described in Genesis 28, where the Patriarch "saw, in his sleep, a ladder standing upon earth, and the top thereof touching heaven. . . . And the Lord leaning upon the ladder, saying to him, *I am the Lord God of Abraham,* thy father, and the *God of Isaac.* . . . And when Jacob awaked out of sleep, he said: Indeed *the Lord is in this place,* and I knew it not. . . . And Jacob arising in the morning took the stone, which he had laid under his head, and set it up for a title, pouring oil upon the top of it. And he called the City Bethel. . . . And he made a vow," etc.

311. In Exod. 13:21, one of the incidents of the flight out of Egypt is described as follows: "And *the Lord* went before them to show the way, by day in a pillar of cloud, and by night in a pillar of fire: that he might be the guide of their journey at both times." And, in the next chapter (14) this same divine Guide, shown in Chap. 13 to have been *the Lord,* is spoken of (verse 19) as "the Angel of God";

"And *the Angel of God*, who went before the camp of Israel, removing went behind them; and together with him the pillar of cloud, leaving the forepart."

312.   Judges 2:1, *et seq.*, records the going up of the Angel of the Lord from Galgal to the place of weepers; and this Angel speaks of Himself clearly as God. "*I made you* go out of Egypt, and have brought you into the land, for which *I swore* to your fathers, and *I promised* that *I would* not make void *my covenant* with you forever," etc.

313.   In the history of Gedeon, Judges 6:12 to 21, it is related that the Angel of the Lord appeared to him, and said: "the Lord is with thee, O most valiant of men," etc. Gedeon, answering, addressed the Angel as "Lord" and "my Lord," and offered sacrifice to Him, and then the Angel vanished. Whereupon we are further told: "Gedeon, seeing that it was *the Angel of the Lord*, said: Alas, my Lord, God; for I have seen *the Angel of the Lord* face to face; and the Lord said to him: Peace be with thee; fear not, thou shalt not die." Verses 22, 23.

314.   This fear on the part of Gedeon, that he was to die, may be understood by referring to Exod. 33:20: "And again he (God) said: Thou canst not see my face; for man shall not see me and live." [1]

"And," it is further said, in Judges 6:24, "Gedeon built there an altar *to the Lord* and called it *the Lord's peace* (Jehova-Shalom), until this present day," etc.

[1] The reference here is evidently to seeing God in all His glory, for this divine announcement is in reply to the request of Moses that he be allowed to see the glory of God. "And he said: Show me thy glory." Exod. 33:18.

315. We have, in Judges, Chap. 13, the case, also, of Manue, upon whom came the same fear as had come upon Gedeon. The chapter last cited relates the appearance of the Angel of the Lord to Manue's wife, foretelling the birth to her of a son, Samson, and prescribing the preparations to be made for the coming event. Later, the *Angel of the Lord* was seen by both husband and wife. And a sacrifice was offered; "and when the flame from the altar went up toward heaven, the *Angel of the Lord* ascended also in the flame," verse 20. Before this, both Manue and his wife had thought that it was a man of God who was speaking to them (verses 6, 8, 10, 11) and Manue "knew not that it was *the Angel of the Lord.*" Verse 16. But when the One Whom they had supposed to be simply "a man of God," was seen rising to Heaven upon the flame of the sacrifice; forthwith Manue understood that it was an [1] *Angel of the Lord,* and he said to his wife: "we shall certainly die, *because we have seen God.*" Verses 21, 22.

316. Now, unless the Angel of the Lord, thus mentioned throughout Judges, Chap. 13, was God, there is no truth in Manue's declaration that he and his wife had *"seen God"*; and, moreover, various parts or passages of this chapter are conflicting.

317. It cannot be logically held, as some attempt to do, that the Angel of the Lord, as spoken of in so

---

[1] The Douay translation again uses, as does, also, the King James Edition, "an" instead of "the" in this connection, where the Vulgate leaves it open, of course, to use either of the articles: "Statimque intellexit Manue, Angellum Domini esse." The Revised Version, however, gives "the Angel of the Lord."

many Scriptural passages, refers only to so many theophanies, or self-manifestations of God. To maintain this is to contend that the name, Angel of the Lord, as used in the Sacred Writings, does not apply to any person or being at all, but is a mere designation of a particular shape or form, or disguise, assumed on occasions by the great Jehova, in His dealings with men.

318.   Were such a theory correct, a fact so important would have been specially mentioned somewhere in the Sacred Books, either in the Old Testament, or in the New; it would scarcely have been left to mere surmise.   Conceding, for the sake of argument only, the truth of this theory; is it to be supposed that even one writer should several times recur to this same subject, without stating that, after all, "Angel of the Lord" was not a proper name, but was a mere designation of a particular mask or disguise?   And, when several Sacred Writers have dealt, each more or less frequently, with this same subject, are we to believe that not one of their number foresaw that interpreters, during their own or during succeeding ages, would construe what they had written, as indicating that the Angel of the Lord is a divine Person?

319.   But, there is no ambiguity here.   The *Angel of the Lord*, as we have seen, is spoken of as God, in numerous scriptural passages, and as Himself acting and speaking directly.   Here, as elsewhere, the literal meaning must be preferred.

320.   We may understand how God, being a pure Spirit, hence invisible to corporeal eyes, found it

necessary, when appearing to man, to assume some
visible form. But the fact of such an appearance
would be expressed by fitting words, such as "the
Lord appeared, . . . in the form of an Angel,"
or "in the form of a man," as the case might be. The
fact is that Holy Writ does not say, in any of the
cases considered above, that it was God, under the
form of an Angel, who spoke or acted; and it does
say, or show, very positively, that it was the *Angel
of the Lord* who spoke or acted, and that He is God.

321. Furthermore, the Angel of the Lord is
presented to us in several passages of Holy Writ as
speaking or acting, without an actual appearance to
any person. When Agar was in the Wilderness of
Bersabee, with her infant, Ismael, the Angel of the
Lord did not make himself visible, but only called to
her "from heaven." And God heard the voice of the
boy and "the [1] *Angel of God called to Agar.*" etc.
Gen. 21:17. Jacob, telling Rachel and Lia of the
command which God had given to him to leave the
house of Laban, does not say that he saw the *Angel
of God;* "And the Angel of God *said to me* in my
sleep," etc. Gen. 31:11. When Abraham was prevented from sacrificing his son, Isaac, it was the
Angel of the Lord who "from heaven called to him"
and prevented this sacrifice. See, also, Gen. 22:15.

322. We have seen how the Israelites were guided
through the desert by the Angel of God; and we are
also expressly told that the Angel of God, in render-

[1] For reasons already stated, we translate here, "vocavitque
Angelus Dei," by "and the Angel of God called," and not by
"And an Angel," etc., as is to be found in the Douay Version.

ing this service, appeared "by day in a pillar of cloud and by night in a pillar of fire." Exod. 13:21, 22, with 14:19, 20. Now, if "the Angel of God" was a mere disguise assumed by Jehova when appearing to men, "the pillar of cloud" in the case under immediate consideration, and "the pillar of fire" were mere guises of a guise; a proposition that would be utterly absurd.

323. Exod. 23:20, *et seq.*, shows very clearly the actual personality of the Angel of God: "Behold I will send my Angel, who shall go before thee in thy journey, and bring thee in the place I have prepared. Take notice of him and hear his voice, and do not think him one to be contemned; for he will not forgive when thou hast sinned, and *my name is in him.*[1]

324. The Jewish Rabbinical Writers disagreed very much among themselves upon a great variety of topics. Moreover, they wrote, many of them at least, under the fear that their compositions might fall into

---

[1] *"My* name is in him." God is often spoken of in the Old Testament and by Jewish commentators, as "the Name" or "My Name." "And when he had blasphemed the Name and cursed it, he was brought to Moses." Lev. 24:11. "If thou wilt not . . . fear his glorious and terrible name; that is, the Lord, thy God," etc. Deut. 28:58. Aben-Ezra, commentary on the thirty-third chapter of Exodus says: "Moses demanded to see *the Name* and *the Name* answered him, a man in this life cannot see me." A few lines above in the same commentary: "In my opinion the true exposition of the sense of this passage is as follows: *The Name* having said to Moses, verse 2, 'I will send an Angel before thee,' he answered him, verse 13, 'You have not made known to me who is the one whom you will send with me, if it is him of whom it is written, for my *Name is in him?* And *the Name* answered him, it is indeed me, in my proper essence who will march before you." Other Rabbinical testimonies to the same effect could be quoted if needed. Drach, *De l'Harmonie entre l'Eglise et la Synagogue,* Vol. I, p. 408.

the hands of the Gentiles and supply the latter with arguments in favor of the divinity of Jesus Christ. Nevertheless, out of the confusion of their writings may be drawn an abundance of evidence, proving that the Older Hebrews applied the names Angel of Jehova, Angel of the Covenant, etc., to the Messiah, and proof also that the Messiah was regarded among them as the Son of God.

325. Aben Ezra, in his Commentary on Ozee (Hosea) 12, says: "God revealed to Moses the name of the Angel, who spoke to our Patriarch (Jacob). He informed him that *it is the God of Angels, object of their adoration.* It is for this reason that his memorial (Osee 12:5) is Jehova."

326. R. David Kimhi, on Mal. 3:1, "The Lord, whom you seek. This is the King Messiah. And he is also the Angel of the Covenant."

327. And Abarbanel: "God said, concerning the redemption of his people: And presently the Lord whom you seek shall come to his temple. For he will be the King Messiah, and he will be the Angel of the Covenant, who will establish on earth the covenant of peace. Thereby he designates the Venerated Name (God) who shall then come into the sanctuary, which shall be within his temple; and his glory, his essence (schechina) will there abide. And he calls him Lord (Adon), because he is Lord (Adon) of all the earth."

328. Medracsh-Rabba, section *mischpatim,* toward the end: "God said to Moses: He who guarded the fathers will also guard the children. It is thus that Abraham blesses his Son, Isaac, saying

to him: Jehova, God of Heaven . . . will send his
Angel before thee.   Jacob, our father, says to his
children: the Angel that has delivered me from all
evil will bless these young boys (Gen. 48:16), that is
to say it is he who has delivered me from the hand of
Esau and from the hand of Laban.   The same provided in the times of famine for my sustenance and
for all my other needs.   God said to Moses, my Divinity will manifest itself in all places, where this
Angel will show himself; for it is written: And the
Angel of Jehova appeared to him in a flame of fire,
in the midst of a bush (Exod. 3:2).[1]   And immediately after it is said 'And when Jehova saw that he
went forward to see, God called to him, out of the
midst of the bush, saying to him,' etc. (same verse
4).   And every time that the Children of Israel shall
invoke this Angel, they shall obtain their salvation.
Thus happened it at the bush, for it is said: 'For the
cry of the Children of Israel is come unto me' (same
verse 9).   Thus happened it also with Gedeon, 'And
the Angel of Jehova came and sat under an oak, that
was in Ophra. . . .   And Jehova answered him:
Go in this thy strength and thou shalt deliver Israel
from the hand of Madian; Know that I have sent
thee.'   So shall it be in the future time, at the coming
of the Messiah.   When *that Angel* will appear, salvation will come to Israel; for it is written: 'Behold

---

[1] The Vulgate has here "Apparuitque ei Dominus in flamma
ignis, de medio rubi;" that is, "the Lord appeared," etc.   The
Hebrew text, as shown above, makes it the Angel of Jehova,
who so appeared.   Acts 7:30 reads "Apparuit illi in deserto
montis Sina, Angelus in igna flammæ rubi;" and verses 31,
et seq., clearly show that this angel was God.

I send my Angel, and he shall prepare the way before me.' "

329. R. Moses Nahhmenides, on Exod. 23:21: "And here is the explanation according to the way of truth: The Angel who is promised here is the Angel Redeemer, who includes in himself the great name of God, with which *He has created the worlds*. He is the angel who said to Jacob *I am the God of Bethel* (Gen. 31:11, 13), that is to say of the house of God; for the custom of Kings is to inhabit their palaces. Scriptures call him Angel because *all the government of the World belongs to this Mode of the Divinity*. And our doctors teach that it is Metatron. So long as this Angel was in the midst of Israel, God, whose name is in him, was found in the midst of this people. But, after the sin of the golden calf, He wished to *withdraw the presence of His Divinity* from the midst of the Hebrews and to give them for a guide one of the Angels whom He sends ordinarily (Exod. 33:2, *et seq.*); Moses obtained by his prayer *the return of the divine Glory*."

330. R. Behhai, Commentary on Exodus 33: "And God said, I will send my angel before thee. 'My Angel' means my Angel well-beloved, Him by Whom I am known in the World. It is in speaking of this Angel that God said to Moses: '*My Face shall go*,' when Moses made this prayer: 'Show me now thy way,' which means, show me the mode by which you are known in the World. And God answered him: My *Face* shall go. Such is also the meaning of this verse: And '*the Angel of His Face* has saved them' (Isa. 63:9), that is to say the Angel *Who is*

His Face itself. And our doctors (Sanhedrin, fol. 38, verso) have explained in the following manner, verse 21 of Chap. 23 of Exodus: *Do not think that* this Angel is God to my exclusion, for it must be considered that all *enters into unity,* that all is *absorbed in unity, without any division.* Thou shalt not disobey him. For he who disobeys him, disobeys my *name One* which is in Him. And if in connection with these words of David, 'For with thee is pardon, O Adonai' (Psa. 129 (130):4) our doctors have said that God has not given to any angel the power to remit sins,[1] this *must not be understood except of Angels separated from the Divine Essence.* 'And you shall do all what I shall speak' God does not say here what he (the Angel) shall speak, but what I shall speak, this to announce that the *voice* of this Angel is the *Word of God.* He who sends inspires, and He who is sent is inspired. *For this one emanates from God, the same as in the creation of the lower world woman emanates* from man as it is written: 'She shall be called Isscha (woman) because she was taken out of Isch (man).' Gen. 2:23. . . . And when the Children of Israel committed the sin of the golden calf this Angel withdrew from among them as God had said: 'For I will not go up in the midst of thee' (Exod. 33:3). For, so long as this Angel, in whom is the Name One, went in the midst of Israel God would not say: 'For I will not go up in

---

[1] We are told by Saint Mark 2:3, *et seq.,* how Christ healed "one sick of the palsy," saying to him: "Son, thy sins are forgiven thee." And "some of the scribes sitting there were thinking in their hearts: Why does this man speak thus? He blasphemeth. Who can forgive sins but God only?"

the midst of thee'; his *Name* being in the midst of the people, *and he being there personally.* But when *God*, blessed be his name, *withdrew from them*, because of their sin, He wished that one of his Angels, *Separated from His essence* should be sent as their guide. This is what the verse says: 'And I will send an angel . . . for I will not go up in the midst of thee.' "

331. Moses, Nahhmenides, discussing the words of Moses to Jehova "And thou dost not let me know, whom thou wilt send with me" (Exod. 33:12) says further: "Moses desired to know if it was the Angel which God had already announced to him (ib. 23:20), the Angel in whom is the divine Name. And the meaning of this reply of God, the Holy, blessed be He, *'my face shall go'* is equivalent, according to all the commentators, to: *I myself shall go.* Nevertheless this passage will remain always unintelligible for whomsoever that is ignorant *of the mysteries of the Holy Scriptures.* And I consider that Moses desired to know the *Unity such as it is in Jehova.* Then God, the Holy, blessed be He, answered him *My Face shall go*, that is *the Angel of the Testament*, for whom you demand (Mal. 3:1), for in Him my Face manifests itself, and it is of Him that it is written: *Behold what Jehova says, in an acceptable time I have heard thee* (Isa. 49:8). *For my name is in Him.*"

CHAPTER XI.

THE SPIRIT OF GOD.

332. WE FIND in the Gospels more frequent and plainer references to God the Holy Ghost than we do in the Old Testament; and yet, even in the Gospels [1] there is no attempt at any formal definition in this regard. In Matt. 28:19, the Apostles are commissioned to teach all nations "baptizing them in the name of the *Father*, and of the *Son* and of the *Holy Ghost*." The Three Divine Persons are named here consecutively and placed upon a plane of association and equality; but, unmistakable as the implication is, here as to the divine nature of the Holy Spirit, there is in this text no *direct* assertion of this great fact. Though, in John 14:16, 17, and 15:26, there is the promise given of another Paraclete to come, the Spirit of Truth and evidently the equal of the Son, Who was the first Paraclete, yet the equality of the two is not expressly announced.

333. Holy Scripture tells of the baptism of our

[1] We say here "the Gospels," and thus exclude I John 5:7, which contains the celebrated "Comma Joanneum," or text of "the Three Heavenly Witnesses." This is done, not for the reason that there is controversy over the authenticity of this passage, but because, its appearance being late, its presence does not militate against the suggestion that, when the gospels were written, the people, at least such among them as were deeply versed in the Scriptures and in the sacred traditions, had a knowledge of the nature and mission of God, the Holy Ghost, sufficiently clear to render any precise and positive definition thereof not urgent.

Lord in the Jordan by Saint John. "And Jesus being baptized," Saint Matthew says, 3:16, 17, "went up presently out of the water; and behold the heavens were opened to him; and he saw the Spirit of God descending as a dove, and coming upon him. And behold a voice from heaven, saying: this is my beloved Son, in whom I am well pleased." [1] Here we have a very clear indication of the Trinity,[2] but still it is not said, in plain words, that "the Spirit of God" is one of three Divine Persons, constituting the one and only God.

334. This omitting to define, positively, in the Gospels, the nature of the Third Person of the Holy Trinity, while at the same time ascribing to Him acts and works, and showing Him in situations, all bespeaking his Personality and Divinity, may be reasonably accounted for on the theory that the sacred truth of the Trinity was known, even in those early days, to "men of good will."

335. When Moses and Aaron approached Pharaoh, demanding in the name of Jehova the liberation of their brethren, the Egyptian put to them this question: "Who is Jehova, that I should hear his voice and let Israel go?" Exod. 5:1, 2. On the other hand, the Gospel of Saint Matthew (1:19, 20) tells how Joseph was at one time troubled in mind and thinking to put the Blessed Virgin away pri-

[1] See, also, Mark 1:10, 11; Luke 3:22; II Peter 1:17.

[2] The "Spirit of God" is mentioned in this passage as, in the form of a dove, "coming down upon Him;" that is, upon the Son, while the Father in heaven speaks the words from heaven, "This is my beloved Son," etc. Thus all three take part, as distinct persons, in one and the same occurrence, or event.

vately, and how "the Angel of the Lord appeared to him in his sleep, saying: Joseph Son of David, fear not . . . for that which is conceived in her is of the Holy Ghost, etc." And Joseph did not inquire of the Angel: "Who is the Holy Ghost?" From this it may be inferred that the Foster Father of the Savior already had knowledge with regard to the nature of God the Holy Ghost.[1]

336. The Spirit of God is early mentioned in the Old Testament. The first verse of Genesis tells that "In the beginning, God created heaven and earth." The second verse, after declaring that "the earth was void and empty and darkness was upon the face of the deep," adds: "And the *Spirit of God* moved over the waters."

337. It is apparent that the passages indicate a distinction of some kind between "God" and "the Spirit of God"; otherwise, why should the Sacred Writer have introduced the two names in such close and immediate connection? It was not for rhetorical effect, as to avoid tautology, for the name of God is repeated with great frequency and closeness in the succeeding verses, as in other parts of the older Scriptures.

338. The "Spirit of God" has here its own predicate "moved over the waters"; and, in the preceding verse, the nominative "God" is found also with a predicate of its own: "God created heaven and earth." The actions described in the two verses under consideration are not alike in their natures, and

---

[1] See Chevalier P. B. L. Drach: *De l'Harmonie entre l'Eglise et la Synagogue,* Vol. I, p. 279.

the difference between them confirms the conclusion that the Actors named are distinct.

339.   Indeed, if "the Spirit of God," as mentioned in Gen. 1 :2, be not a distinct Person, performing His particular part in the work of perfected creation, the paragraph in question has much the appearance of having been interpolated, and there is in every case a presumption against the theory of interpolation, unless there be strong proof in support of it.   Accept, however, the dogma of the Holy Trinity, and the mention here of the "Spirit of God" as moving over the waters, following immediately after the statement that "God" created the earth "void and empty" becomes intelligible.

340.   It is not easy to define with certainty what is meant in Gen. 1 :2, by the expression "moved over the waters."   The word "waters," as here used, has evidently not the sense that belongs to it when found in verses 9, 10, of the same chapter, which tell of the waters of this globe being drawn together into seas, and of the continents being established.   Gen. 1 :2, presents to us its "waters" as "void and empty," as a "deep"; whereas, when the land rose up from the flood, this earth was no longer in the form of a "deep," no longer "empty and void."   The word "moved" is scarcely employed here in the sense of mere locomotion or in that of a shifting or changing of position or place, or relation, as when winds blow over the surface of the sea.   It more probably has the meaning of "inciting to action," "causing to act" [1]

---

[1] See *Standard Dictionary* (Funk & Wagnalls).   Vo. Move., Definitions 2, 5.

and in this sense suggests that the Spirit of God, operating in or upon the original chaos, either directly or by endowing it with certain potentialities, brought it into eventual order and shape and subjected it to those physical laws which now control the universe.[1]

341.   Following this line of interpretation, since the Holy Ghost is God, we may read verses 3, *et seq.*, of this same chapter (Genesis 1) as a strict continuation of this paragraph: "The Spirit of God moved over the waters."   And the numerous divine operations detailed in said verses 3, *et seq.*, may be justly regarded as being all in the direction of developing or perfecting the primordial chaos and reducing it to system and order; the making of light, the separation of the waters, the establishment of the continents, the forming of living things, etc.

342.   These sacred texts, thus read, present to us the Spirit of God as a divine and operating Person; and they furnish, also, a description, in general terms, of the line of his particular work, in the fashioning of our universe.

343.   To those who reject the Trinity these inspired passages must appear inharmonious and confusing.   They deny the plurality of Persons in the Unity of God; how then shall they logically maintain,

---

[1] The force of this reasoning is not affected by changing the word "moved," in our paragraph, to "brooded," or to "hovered," or to "fluttered"; for, whatever may be the manner in which the Spirit of God held himself above the waters, His presence there must have been for some definite purpose.   And the nature of that purpose is not altered by the character of the Latin or English terms which may be chosen to represent, in translations, the verb of the original text.

in presence of the preposition "of," that "God" and the "Spirit of God" as used in the passage quoted, are merely different names for absolutely one and the same Divine Person? The preposition "of," as found in our phrase, "the Spirit of God" is not to be ignored. It makes of this term, as it were a partitive, showing "the Spirit of God" as one only of the three Divine Persons, in the Unity of God. If not so, then "the Spirit" here is some part of God, or one of His possessions.

344. Either of these two conclusions as to the province of the preposition "of" in the clause we are considering, is fatal to the theory that the "God" and the "Spirit of God," as appearing in our text, are only different names for one and the same divine Person. Upon the same principle, as here, when we speak of the "Soul of Man" we do not express the same thought as when we say simply "Man"; and the servant or the friend of a man is certainly distinct from the man himself.

345. Unitarians may choose here between these difficulties. If the Spirit of God be part only of the Almighty, what part is it, and what are the divine parts not included? What, under such a theory, becomes of the unity and indivisibility of God? If the Spirit of God is some creature, such as an angel or a higher spirit of any sort, why should a creature be participator in the supreme work of making or fashioning a universe? And, if moving over the waters does not mean developing or perfecting the original chaos, but suggests only locomotion or movement on the part of some subordinate being, why this

break into the solemn narrative of the doings of God himself, in order merely to declare that some finite thing, for no defined purpose, "moved over the waters"? [1]

346.   The Spirit of God is mentioned, in other passages of the Old Testament, in connection with creative work. In Job 33:4, it is said: "The Spirit of God made me, and the breath of the Almighty [2] gave me life." In Psa. 32 (33) :6, we find: "By the word of the Lord the heavens were established; and all the power of them by the Spirit of his Mouth." In Psa. 103 (104) :30: "Thou shalt send forth thy Spirit and they shall be created; and thou shalt redeem the face of the earth."

347.   We read in the New Testament of the descent of the Holy Ghost upon the Apostles and Disciples on the first Pentecost Sunday:

"And suddenly there came a sound from heaven, as of a mighty wind coming, and it filled the whole house where they were sitting; and there appeared to them cloven tongues as it were of fire, and it sat upon each of them; and they were all filled with the Holy Ghost," etc.   Acts 2:2, 3, 4.

348.   Saint Paul says: "Or know ye not that your

[1] We have already discussed along somewhat different lines, this same subject in the preceding chapter, entitled "In the Head of the Book." In that former chapter, good reasons, we think, are advanced for maintaining that the "Spirit of God," as found in our text, does not refer to air in motion, or, in other words, to the wind.

[2] Where, in any of the versions, in any of these texts, the expression is found "the breath of His mouth," or "the breath of the Almighty," the meaning is the same as the "Spirit of God." See *Dictionary of the Bible* (Hastings), Vo. Spirit; also Vo. Holy Spirit.

members are the Temple of the Holy Ghost who is
in you, whom you have from God; and you are not
your own?" I Cor. 6:19.[1] And, in numerous passages of the Gospels, of the Acts and of the Epistles,
we read of holy men and women, who were "filled
with the Holy Spirit." Saint John the Baptist, for
instance, was "filled with the Holy Ghost, even from
his Mother's womb." [2] Luke 1:15. Elizabeth (Luke
1:47), Zachary (Luke 1:67), Peter (Acts 4:8) and
Paul (Acts 13:9) were also "filled with the Holy
Ghost"; and all the Apostles and Disciples, as well,
who were assembled together on the first Pentecost
Sunday, Acts 2:4.

349. This presence of the Holy Ghost in men has
shown itself, under the New Law, in the power given
to chosen individuals to perform miracles and to accomplish important works. Similarly, under the Old
Law, there were frequent instances, where the Spirit
of God moved particular men to the doing of extraordinary things. Bezeleel was filled with the Spirit
of God, that he might shape perfectly the gold, silver
and brass that was to go in or upon the tabernacle.
Exod. 37:2, *et seq.* Joseph, in Egypt, was similarly
inspired by the Holy Ghost. Gen. 41:38. The Seventy Ancients received Him when they were appointed. Num. 11:25. Othoniel (Judges 3:10),
Jepthe (Judges 11:29), Gideon (Judges 6:34),
David (II Kings (II Sam.) 23:2); all of these and

---

[1] See, also, I Cor. 3:16, 17; II Cor. 6:16.

[2] It is worthy of mention that the Prophet Jeremiah also en-
joyed this same great privilege: "Before I formed thee in the
bowels of thy Mother, I knew thee, and before thou camest
from the womb, I sanctified thee." Jer. 1:5.

others were impelled in what they said or did by the Spirit of God.

350.   We should note carefully this similarity in the operations of the Holy Spirit, in particular men, under both Dispensations, as going to show that both Testaments, Old and New disclose identically the same concept as to the Spirit of God.   And, in order that this identity of the Holy Ghost, as spoken of or referred to in both Testaments, be made to appear more clearly, we may usefully continue our comparisons of what is written, in this regard, in both of the Sacred Books.

351.   When the Holy Ghost came down upon the Apostles and Disciples, on Pentecost, the first external result recorded is that "they began to speak with divers tongues, according as the Holy Ghost gave them to speak."   Acts 2:4.   Elizabeth (Luke 1:41, 42), and Zachary (same, verses 67, *et seq.*) were both of them filled with the Holy Ghost, and each was moved to proclaim or affirm some of the great truths of Christian faith.   And when it was made known to Zachary that his son, to be born, was to be "filled with the Holy Ghost from its Mother's womb," the Angel added: "He shall convert many of the children of Israel to the Lord, their God." Luke 1:15, 16.   The Savior, Himself once said to the Apostles: "Be not thoughtful beforehand what ye shall speak; but whatsoever shall be given to you in that hour, that speak ye: For it is not you that speak, but the Holy Ghost."   Mark 13:11.

352.   From the passages above quoted, and others

which might be added, it appears that, under the New Dispensation, one of the great works of the Holy Ghost is to bring to the minds of men knowledge of the Gospel. Christianity is the culmination, the perfection of Ancient Judaism. St. Paul says in connection with the Old Covenant and its ceremonials: "Which are a shadow of the things to come, but the body is of Christ." Col. 2:17. And the Savior, Himself has said: "Do not think that I am come to destroy the law and the prophets. I am not come to destroy but to fulfill," etc. Matt. 5:17.[1]

353. Under the Old Dispensation, the attention of men was drawn, in different ways, to great spiritual events that were to come. Under the New, however, the major part of these great events have become accomplished facts, the Incarnation, the Atonement and Redemption, the Resurrection of Christ, the Foundation of the Christian Church, etc. Therefore it was that before the advent of Christ, the work of the Holy Spirit, so far as concerned the making known of religious truth, was to a large extent, predictive prophecy.[2] On the other hand, how-

[1] Saint Augustine says, on this subject: "The same religion which we now call the Christian Religion, was the one of the ancient centuries. Already its dominion had lasted from the days of our first Parents, when the Word was made flesh and manifested himself to the world. This event brought with itself, actually, no change other than a new denomination. The true faith, therefore, which had existed from the earliest times, began then to be called the Christian Religion, to the end that it might be announced to all the earth that Christ, in order to open for us the Kingdom of Heaven, came to accomplish the law and the Prophets, far from abolishing them." Retract. 1; 13:3°.

[2] "For prophecy came not from the will of man at any time; but the holy men of God spoke, inspired by the Holy Ghost."

ever, since the establishment of the Church of Christ, the mission of the Spirit of God, as regards the dissemination of "all truth," is to proclaim the perfection of the Old Law and fulfilment, in principal part at least, of the Old Testament prophecies and promises.

354. The New Testament was written, most of it certainly, by men who were of the Jewish nation, and their very writings show, at the least, that they were men of observation and intelligence. With the exception of Saint Paul and Saint Luke, all had personally followed Christ, as, during his public ministry, He passed from place to place, through Judea, preaching and teaching; and, with the two exceptions noted, they had listened to the words of the Savior, as they fell from His very lips. While following Christ in person, and, subsequently, while themselves preaching and teaching, they must have engaged in very many religious discussions among themselves and with friends and against opponents. Holy Scripture shows the Redeemer, Himself, and the Apostles after him, as appealing often to the Old Law, including the prophecies, in confirmation of what was either being said or written. If in writing as they have done concerning the Holy Ghost, these inspired Authors were introducing a dogma absolutely new, some one or more of their number would have apologized, in some way, for the innovation, and explained with positive definiteness its meaning to a people that had not theretofore been at all ac-

II Peter 1:21; I Cor. 14:2; Dan. 2:28. The creed says of the Spirit of God: "Who spoke by the prophets."

quainted with it. Or there would have been mention somewhere, of criticisms or protests against it from Scribes and Pharisees, or from other unbelieving Jews.[1]

355. For the reasons above detailed, we may well insist that, in the work of interpreting the Old Testament, our first and most confident recourse should be to the pages of the New. Therefore, even were it a fact that the Rabbinical writers have made no mention of the Spirit of God in the Talmud, or in any of their other commentaries, we might well attribute their silence in this regard to unwillingness on their part to confirm in any way the Christian dogma of the Trinity; and we might place entire reliance, in this connection, in the earlier testimony of the Apostles.

356. But the Rabbinical writers have not maintained a strict silence upon this subject. Clear references, by modern Rabbis, to the Holy Ghost, are to be found, particularly in discussions and explanations concerning the incommunicable Name of God. We shall not, however, furnish here any Rabbinical quotations taken from discussions and explanations of the character last referred to, as such quotations will find more fitting place in special study devoted to that most deep and interesting subject, the mystical meaning of the Ineffable Name, Jehova. Ex-

---

[1] It is recorded that, when the Saviour spoke for the first time to his followers, of the mystery of the Holy Eucharist, some of his Disciples said: "This saying is hard, and who can hear it." John 6:61. And again it is written: "After this, many of his Disciples went back and walked no more with him." John 6:67.

cluding, therefore, for the time being, all extracts from the Rabbins, bearing in any particular way upon the Divine Nature, as mytically suggested in that form of God's name which the Jews so deeply revered, we still find, in Rabbinical writings, other references to the Holy Spirit, some of which it may be useful to quote here.

357.   The Holy Spirit is not to be confused with the Shekina (that which dwells or resides), concerning which latter (the Shekina) Modern Jews present different conceptions.   Yoma, fol. 21, col. 2, mentions five things as absent from the second temple, which had been present in the first: (1) the Ark, the Mercy Seat and the Cherubim; (2) the fire from heaven on the altar; (3) the Visible Presence (Shekina); (4) the Holy Spirit; (5) the Urim and Thummim.

358.   In the same book (Yoma, fol. 78, col. 2), it is said: "A priest who does not speak by the Holy Spirit, and upon whom the Shekina does not rest, should not speak oracularly."

359.   And in Beracoth, fol. 31, col. 2: "Some think . . . that Hannah spoke in the following sense: Thou are neither lord, nor does the Holy Spirit rest upon thee, because thou doest suspect me in this matter, and hast formed an uncharitable opinion of me. . . . Neither the Shekina, nor the Holy Spirit are with thee."

360.   The three passages just quoted indicate that the Holy Spirit and the Shekina were regarded as distinct; and they go to show more clearly, by their differentiation, the idea of a separate personality for the Spirit of God.

361.   "In the West (Palestine) they construed it (Amos 5:2) thus: 'She has fallen, and will fall no more; rise virgin of Israel.'   Rav. Nachman bar Ytzchak said: 'All the same David raises them through the Holy Spirit,' as it is said (Psa. 144 (145):14, 'the Lord lifteth up all that fall.' "   Beracloth, fol. 4, col. 2.

362.   "It was clear then, that Rabbon Gamaliel was under the influence of the Holy Spirit; and his conduct inculcated three lessons," etc.   Eiruvin, fol. 64, col. 2.

363.   "On the death of the last prophets, Haggai, Zechariah and Malachi, the Holy Spirit departed from Israel; but they were still availing themselves of the daughter (Echo) of a voice" (for the reception of divine communications).   Yoma, fol. 9, col. 2.

364.   "Iscah (Gen. 11:29) is another name for Sarai.   She was so called, because she spoke intuitively by the Holy Spirit; as is said (ibid, 21:12): "In all Sarah saith unto thee, hearken to her voice."   Meguillah, fol. 14, col. 1.

365.   Puah (Exod. 1:15) is another name for Miriam.   She was so called, because, prompted by the Holy Ghost, she used to say: "My Mother will give birth to a son, who will save Israel."   (Puah signifies to call out.)   Soteh, fol. 2, col. 2.

366.   "Rabbi Pinchas ben Yair said . . . holiness leads to (acquisition of) the Holy Spirit, the Holy Spirit leads to resurrection from the dead," etc.   Avodah-zarah, fol. 20, col. 2.[1]

[1] See Hershon's *Genesis, with a Talmudical Commentary* (Sam'l Bagster & Sons, London, Publishers). P. 16, *et seq.*

CHAPTER XII.

THE INEFFABLE NAME—JEHOVA.

367. THE Jews have several names in the Hebrew language for God: Jehova, Ehye, El, Elohim, Elyon (Most High), El Shaddai (God Almighty), Adon, Adonai, etc. But among all the divine names there is one, *Jehova*, most excellent, and which was reserved and incommunicable. By this is meant that, while the other divine appellations might, at times, be otherwise applied, this great name was the exclusive property of the One true God.

368. In the Book of Wisdom, Chap. 14, the origin of idolatry is described, and, in verse 21 of that chapter, it is said: "And this was the occasion of deceiving human life; for men, serving either their affection or their kings, gave *the Incommunicable Name* to stones and wood."

369. In Psa. 82 (83):19 (18), it is written: "And let them know that the Lord (Jehova, in the Hebrew) is thy name; thou alone are the most high over all the Earth." [1] The *"thy"* here is entitled to emphasis, as expressive of exclusive right or title; for by so reading it, we place this passage in line with Wisdom 14:21, as quoted above, and with

[1] The King James Version reads: "That men may know that thou, whose name alone is Jehova art the most high over all the earth." The Revised Version is nearer, in its rendition, to the Douay, but it places the King James Variant in the margin.

182

numerous other texts and authorities which will be referred to later.

370.   Very similar, in its import, is the passage from Isa. 42:8: "I am *Jehova*, this is my name," etc. Here the "*my*" should be likewise held as expressive of exclusive right or possession.

371.   In Num. 6:22 to 26, Aaron and his sons are commanded, through Moses, to bless the people, with the triple blessing, in the name of Jehova:

"Say to Aaron and his sons: Thus shall you bless the Children of Israel, and you shall say to them:

" 'Jehova [1] bless and keep thee;

" 'Jehova show his face to thee and have mercy on thee;

" 'Jehova turn his countenance to thee and give thee peace.' " [2]

372.   Dealing with the passage just quoted, the Talmud, *Sota*, fol. 37, verso and 38 recto, states that this benediction could be given only in the temple at Jerusalem, and in the sacred language (Hebrew), because in that language only the ven-

---

[1] The English translations, in almost every case, give "the Lord," where the Hebrew text has "Jehova." Of course, in dealing with the subject in hand, we must recur to the original form.

[2] This benediction, with its triple pronouncement of the ineffable Name, like the "Holy, Holy, Holy" of Isa. 6:3, is not without its suggestion of the Trinity: a suggestion which becomes more plain, when we consider the manner in which this benediction was given. The priest blessing the people in the name of Jehova thrice repeated, separated the fingers of his uplifted hand into three divisions. The thumb was one division; the index and the middle or long finger joined together formed the second; while the little finger, with its nearest companion, made the third. Drach, *De l'Harmonie entre l'Eglise et la Synagogue*, Vol. I, p. 379.

erable name included all the virtues and *all the mysteries of the divinity.* And the Ghemara adds: "The text says: '*You shall bless the Children of Israel in these words,*' by which is meant by pronouncing the distinguished [1] name. And so that it should not be considered that the distinguished name is not of rigor, or that it might be replaced by another of the appellative names of God, the text adds: 'And they shall invoke my name,' in order to indicate *the name which is reserved to me exclusively.*"

373.   R. Joseph Albo, in his work *Ikkarim,* of the Foundations of Faith, Part II, Chap. 28, says: "The name written by yode, hay, vau, hay (*JHVH,* Jehova) is called the distinguished name. The meaning is distinguished and separated from all other divine names, in that the latter may sometimes be applied to Angels, to men, whereas the name of four letters is absolutely and in all respects unsuitable to any one other than God, blessed be He, *because it expresses His necessary being.*"

374.   Aben-Ezra, Commentary on Isa. 42:8: "The glorious name *Jehova,* alone is the name proper of God; there is no other in Holy Scripture."

Abarbanel, Commentary on the Pentateuch, fol. 6, col. 1, says: "This signifies the holy name, *Son of four letters,* which is called the distinguished name, in as much as it is *the attribute of God* and is applicable to none but Him."

---

[1] "Distinguished," in the absolute, or fullest sense of the term: exalted above other names, and set unchangeably apart from them all.

375. The name, Jehova, being thus restricted by the Hebrews to God alone, was necessarily the most sacred and revered of all names. *Three times*, in the Temple, on the day of Expiations, the High Priest made a public confession of sin, to Jehova; once for himself, once for all the priests descended from Aaron and once for the people. In each of these *three* public confessions, the name Jehova, came *three times*, and that sacred name was pronounced by the High Priest, each time, loudly and distinctly. The Talmud, treatise *Yoma*, fol. 66, recto makes note of the veneration, shown on such occasions, by priests and people toward the incommunicable name: "And the priests, and the people, who were assisting in the Court, so soon as they heard the ineffable name fall from the lips of the high priest, knelt, prostrated themselves, fell upon the earth and exclaimed: Blessed be the name of the glory of His kingdom (His glorious and majestic name) for all eternity."

376. So great was the veneration in which this particular name of God was held by the Jewish nation, that the common people were forbidden to pronounce it at all; and the priests, also, except on stated occasions, in the temple and as part of the exercise of divine worship.[1] It was called the ineffable name; the term ineffable being here used in its very highest and widest sense: "Incapable of being expressed in words, unspeak-

---

[1] It is probable that the use of the Sacred Name was permitted, also, when the young priests were being instructed in the forms and ceremonies of divine worship and in the mysteries of religion.

able, unutterable, inexpressible, . . . not to be spoken."

377.   The profound reverence of the Hebrews for the most holy name, *Jehova,* accounts for the severity with which the Jewish law treated those who profaned this sacred appellation.   In Lev. 24:10, *et seq.,* we read: "And behold there went out the son of a woman of Israel, whom she had of an Egyptian, among the children of Israel, and fell at words in camp, with a man of Israel.   And when he had blasphemed *the name,* and had cursed it, he was brought to Moses.   .   .   .   And the Lord spoke to Moses saying: Bring forth this blasphemer without the camp, and let them that heard him put their hands upon his head, and let all the people stone him. And thou shalt speak to the Children of Israel: the man that curseth his God shall bear his sin.   And he that blasphemeth *the name of Jehova,* dying let him die; all the multitude shall stone him, whether he be a native or a stranger.   He that blasphemeth the *name of Jehova,* dying let him die."

378.   The Hebrew word, in the original text of Lev. 24:16, rendered "blasphemed" in our English translations, has also the meaning "pronounced." And that portion of the offense of the man, stoned to death, as related in the passage just quoted, and which is described as blaspheming the name, was probably the pronouncing of that sacred name in a high and angry voice.   The Septuagint translates verse 11 of this chapter (24) of Leviticus: "And the son of the Israelite woman *having named the name,* cursed."   And, in the same version, verse 16 is ren-

dered: "He who names the name of the Lord, let him be put to death." [1] The two Targums, of Onkelos and of Jonathan-ben-Uzziel, and the Syriac Version all present these two verses (Lev. 24:11 and 16) in a similar form, only adding to the verb "pronounce" the adverb "clearly" or "distinctly." [2]

379. The second commandment itself lends support to this interpretation of Lev. 24:11 and 16; for that commandment formally forbids the taking of the name "Jehova" in vain: "Thou shalt not take the name of Jehova, thy God, in vain."

380. Be this as it may, certain it is, as already stated above, that, under the Old Dispensation, priests alone could lawfully pronounce the Tetragrammaton, and they could do so only in the Temple. Whenever in reading or reciting from Holy Scripture, or from any other literature, the most sacred name presented itself, that of *Adonai* was substituted for it, except when the reader was one especially authorized to pronounce the ineffable name, and when the occasion also permitted.

381. Our Savior, Himself, observed this custom of His time and nation, using the name *Adonai*, for Jehova, when quoting texts from the Old Testament. When, for example, Christ was carried up by Satan to the pinnacle of the Temple and invited to cast Himself down, he rebuked the evil one by saying: "It is written again, thou shalt not tempt the Lord

[1] See de Levante's *Hexaglot Bible, Greek Text.* Funk & Wagnall, Pub.

[2] See Drach's *De l'Harmonie entre l'Eglise et la Synagogue,* Vol. I, p. 512, *et seq.*

thy God." Matt. 4:7; Luke 4:12. The original Hebrew of the text here given by the Savior reads: "Thou shalt not tempt *Jehova,* thy God." Deut. 6:16. But the Redeemer quoted it, according to the manner of His people; for the Gospels show that He did not use, on this occasion, the name Jehova, but substituted in its place Adonai, or in the Greek *Kurion.* And, when, quoting the first verse of the Psalms *"Dixit Dominus,"* which reads in Hebrew *"Jehova* said to my Lord, sit thou at my right hand," etc., Christ repeated it, "the Lord (*Kurios*) said to my Lord," etc. Matt. 22:44.

382. Philo, in his Life of Moses, writing of the golden plate which the High Priest wore as a diadem, says: "It was graven with the four letters, which those alone had the permission to pronounce and to hear in the sacred ceremonies (or in the Temple) who had ears and tongue purified by wisdom (holiness). This was prohibited to all others in every way and in every place. The theologians call the name Tetragrammaton."

383. And the same author, discussing, in the same work, the case, already referred to above, of him who was stoned to death for a blasphemous utterance of the ineffable Name, adds: "This name, which all but the most virtuous, who had arrived to a consummate degree of sanctity, are forbidden to pronounce, even in benediction."

384. Josephus, Antiquities, Book 2, Chap. 12, par. 4, telling of Moses upon Sinai, furnishes practical evidence of the prevalence in his time of the rule or law, under consideration. "Whereupon," he says,

"God declared to him His holy Name, which had never before been discovered; concerning which it is not lawful for me to say more." [1]

385. Maimonides, in his Commentary on the Mischna, Treatise "Sota," Chap. 7, writes as follows: "What it is necessary for you to know is that it is not permitted, in any manner except in the office of the Temple of Jerusalem, to read or to explain the ineffable Name, which is *yode, hay, vau, hay.* We find an indication of this in the Law of Moses, where it is written (Exod. 20:24): 'In every place where the memory of my name shall be, I will come to thee and bless thee!' Now our doctors have said: Reverse the verse and read it thus: 'In every place where I shall come to thee and bless thee, there only shall I place the memory of my name.' "

386. Scholars may dispute over the lessons that are to be drawn from the facts, with which we are now dealing, but no one can reasonable deny the facts themselves, or hide in any way their striking and most marvelous character.

387. We shall not, at this moment, make any suggestion as to the mystical import of the Tetragrammaton, or seek to explain why it has been so long considered by Hebrews as belonging exclusively to God, and, consequently, held by them in such reverent reserve. At this time we shall merely endeavor to show that the incommunicable and ineffable name, Jehova, was the recognized property of the

---

[1] Josephus refrained from quoting in full the Ten Commandments, though giving their substance; which was, possibly, because the Decalogue itself contains the sacred name of Jehova. Antiquities, Book III, Chap. 5, par. 4.

Expected One and to draw from this fact the conclusion that the Messiah was held by the Olden Jews as divine.

388.   The Prophet Jeremiah clearly gives the ineffable name to the Messiah: "Behold the days come saith Jehova, and I will raise up to David a just branch; and a king shall reign, and shall be wise; and shall execute judgment and justice in the earth. In those days, Juda shall be saved, and Israel shall dwell confidently; and this is the name they shall call him, *Jehova our just One*." [1]   Jer. 23:5, 6.

---

[1] Jer. 33:15, 16, if genuine, is a practical repetition of same, 23:5, 6.   The King James Edition renders the latter, "She (Jerusalem) shall be called the Lord our Righteousness."   The Douay, from the Vulgate, has: "they shall call him, the Lord, our just One."   The Revised Version is: "She shall be called the Lord is our Righteousness."   The last rendition, if correct, does not bestow the ineffable name upon the chief city of the Jews, any more than did the graving of the divine appellation upon the tablets of the Law, and the mention thereon of divine attributes, etc., give the name of God to the tablets themselves.   The form, in the Revised Version of Jer. 33:16, might be harmonized with same 23:6, by holding that the text in question makes of Jerusalem a monument, as it were, commemorating the Messiah, who was the Righteous, or Just One.   It is the same with the several altars mentioned in the Old Testament as having been given combination names, of which names the Tetragrammaton formed part.   Ancient Hebrew altars were extremely simple in construction, and probably for the most part temporary.   Exod. 20:24, 25, 26.   But, if any of the altars, named in the way now in question, were enduring, they were left, as columns or pillars might have been, to commemorate some attribute, or some manifestation of God, or some particular relation of His toward men.   There is no proof that these combination names were used in popular speech, any more than was the name Emmanuel applied popularly to Christ.   And, if generally used, the Jehova in these names was probably pronounced Adonai; or perhaps, Jeho, as in certain personal names.   Combination names of similar character were given to some men who are mentioned in Holy Writ.   These particular human names like those bestowed upon certain

389. Isa. 28:5, says: "In that day Jehova Sabaoth shall be a crown of glory, and a garland of joy to his people." The paraphrase of Jonathan-ben-Uzziel, presents this passage as follows "In that time *the Messiah of Jehova Sabaoth,* shall be," etc. And in referring to Jer. 33:14, 15, 16, the paraphrase has: "In those days, in that time, I will raise to David *the Messiah of Justification.*"

390. The Talmud, Treatise *Baba-Batra,* fol. 79, verso: "R. Samuel, Son of Nahhmeni says, in the name of R. Yohanan: 'The Messiah bears the name of God Himself; for it is written: And behold how they shall call Him, *Jehova, our just One.*'"

391. The Zohar, Part I, fol. 63, col. 251, declares that the continence of Booz brought to him the privilege of numbering among his posterity "the King-Messiah, *bearing the name of God, Himself.*" [1]

392. A line of authorities such as those quoted,

altars, were made to serve each as a testimony to, or a commemoration of something that was an attribute or a possession of God, or that bore some special relation to Him. And these human appellations did not include the entire Tetragrammaton, so as to require in their utterance a full pronunciation of the incommunicable Name. Thus Jonathan was not called Jehova-Nathan, but Jeho-Nathan.

[1] Chevalier Drach, in his work, *De l'Harmonie entre l'Eglise et la Synagogue,* Vol. II, pp. 392, *et seq.,* marshals all of the above Rabbinical texts on this subject. And he presents others equally pertinent and clear: R. Dav. Kimhhi; on the Prophecy of Jeremiah, given above; the same commentator on Psa. 131 (132):17; Medrasch-Thehillim on Psalm 21; same on Psa. 18:21 and on II Sam. 22:51; Medrasch-Rabba on Lamentations, fol. 68, col. 2, Ed. Amsterdam. And he refers, also, to the following Rabbinical authorities, as giving similar testimony: Yalkut-Reubeni, fol. 65.2; Aben-Ezra, comment on Exod. 18:3; Behhai-ben-Ascher, comment on Pentateuch, fol. 112; R. Jos. Albo, Foundations of Faith, L.II, Chap. 18; R. Moses Alschehh on Jer. 33:6.

or referred to above, as going to show that in Olden Judaism the Ineffable Name was recognized as belonging to the Messiah, needs no corroboration. But, if it did need any, it would find it in the fact that, according to Hebrew tradition, all restrictions upon the general use of the Tetragrammaton were to be removed, after the coming of the Christ.

393.   The Name of the Messiah was considered as having existed from all eternity. In Isa. 9:2, 6, it is written: "The people that walked in darkness have seen a great light, . . . for a child is born to us and a son is given to us, and the government is upon his shoulder; and his name will be called Wonderful, Counsellor, God the Mighty, the Father of the World to come, the Prince of Peace." The Aramaic Paraphrase thus puts this passage from Isaiah: "The Prophet says to the house of David: For a child is born to us, a son is given to us, and he *submitted himself* to keep the holy law. And his *name has been before the centuries*, Admirable in Council, God, powerful, existing eternally; Messiah in the days, the peace whereof shall multiply itself, or shall be great upon us."

394.   The Talmud in two places [1] speaks to the same effect: "The name of the Messiah was created before the creation of the world; for it is written: His name is eternal; before the Sun [2] He had the name, the Son, the Begotten." [3]

[1] Pesahhim, fol. 54, recto; Nedarim, fol. 39, verso.

[2] Psa. 71 (72):17: "Let his name be blessed for evermore; his name continueth before the sun."

[3] R. Isaac Arama, commenting on Genesis, Chap. 47, similarly expresses himself: "Thy birth from the womb, is like the dew

395. The glose of Rabbi Niscim, on this Talmud: "This means that, before the creation of the World, God had already determined to form Him (the Messiah), for, without Him, the world could not exist."

396. And the glose of Rabbi R-Samuel Edels, upon the same Talmud, bears witness to two facts with which we are now especially concerned; first, that to the Messiah belongs the ineffable name, and the second, that, when He was come, the divine name, Jehova, was to be free to all. "The sense is," says this glose, "that *from the time of the Messiah*, the Tetragrammaton name, name of the Holy God, blessed be He, *shall be often in the mouths of all people; for the Messiah will also bear this name*, as is taught in the Chapter *Hascephina*.[1] The Messiah, it is there said, *shall be called by the name of the Holy God*, blessed be He; for it is written: '*and behold the name by which He shall be called, Jehova our Justice.*' But, before the sun, which means before the world was created, the name of the Messiah was not exactly the Tetragrammaton name. It was

of the dawn. We find no one, no prophet, who has predicted his birth before his father and mother were born, excepting the Messiah, our Just One. This is what is shown by these words of the text: 'From before the sun his name was the Begotten.' For, even before the creation of the Sun, the name of our Messiah was strong and solid and He was seated at the right hand of God. And this is what the Psalmist also says: 'Sit thou at my right hand!' And His throne was established by grace and He is there seated."

[1] "Hascephina," title of a chapter in the Treatise Baba-Batra of the Talmud. The passage referred to in the quotation above is in the Treatise named, fol. 75, verso. See Drach, *De l'Harmonie entre l'Eglise et la Synagogue,* Vol. II, p. 89.

simply *Yinnon,* name which represents (under another form) the Tetragrammaton; for it is composed of *Yod, vav* and two *nuns,* which hold the place of the two *hays.*" [1]

397. Chapter 12 of Isaiah is one among the briefer chapters of the Old Testament; but there is none worthier than it of careful study, as going to show that Ancient Israel expected a Savior, Who, under the old dispensation, was yet to come; through Whom salvation was to be obtained, in the then future, and Who is God. The commentary *Minha-Ghedola,* referring to verse 4 of this chapter says: "Invoke his name. In the time of the Messiah, the Tetragrammaton name will be pronounced as it is written."

398. Additional references, to the same effect as those given above, might be presented, but to what purpose? What has been given, both from the Old Testament and from Rabbinical writers, is sufficient to establish the following facts:

1. The name *Jehova* was reserved, by the olden Jews, as indeed it continues to be to this day by all, Christians and Jews, to the one true God, alone, and was incommunicable; and it was in ancient times at least withheld from popular use.

2. The Messiah bore, as His own, this same ineffable and incommunicable name; and it was held that all men, after His coming, were to be free to pronounce it, reverently.

---

[1] Writing the consonants only as was done in former times, Yinnon may be set down, in Roman letters, JNVN, while, as we have seen, Jehova stands JHVH.

399. From these facts, as premises, a conclusion should be drawn; since the one exclusive name of God, *Jehova,* belonged to the Messiah, His, likewise, must be the particular quality or nature of God, of which that name is expressive.

400. The reserve in which the Tetragrammaton was held, under the Old Law, can be understood, if we consider that the incommunicable name was so reserved during a long period of spiritual darkness, when one nation alone on earth was keeping alive the flickering torch of faith; that this most sacred name was so to remain in reserve until the coming of "the Expected of the Nations," who was to enlighten and save all mankind.

401. But, behind all this lies another and a deeper problem: Why was this name Jehova chosen from the beginning, among all the divine names, as that particular one which was to be ineffable and incommunicable, and held, under the Old Law, in such rigorous reserve?

402. Undertaking the study of this problem, we find ourselves facing a condition, with regard to this one form of the divine name, which, as already intimated, is striking and marvelous. During thousands of years, through wars, tumults and disasters innumerable, through dispersions, the last of which has endured now going on nineteen hundred years, a remarkable people have held this one particular name of God in strict reserve and in a profound veneration.

403. Some think they solve this problem, when they denounce this time-honored religious practice of the Jews as superstitious. But it is often difficult

to determine justly what is and what is not a superstition. If we can conceive of no reason whatsoever why Israel should have been so very reticent, with regard to the great name Jehova, and so formally reverent toward it, we might put this all down as a vain observance, the most singularly persistent, however, of all vain observances recorded in history. But, rather than presume that a mere superstitious practice has laid a hold, so broad and strong and enduring upon an entire people by no means unintelligent, we must accept any explanation whatsoever that is at all rational, and which saves at the same time the Jewish race from the charge of persistent foolishness in this regard.

404. We must, therefore, search for a serious motive, or reason, perhaps more than one, lying behind this most ancient Jewish usage; either a divine injunction, laid upon the chosen people, or a divine revelation, which came in some way to them. In doing this, we may reasonably begin by supposing that there is attached to the revered name, some mystical meaning connected with the very nature itself of the Almighty.

405. Many have contended that the name Jehova is derived from the Hebrew verb *haya*, meaning to be, or from the unsued form *hava*, with a similar meaning; that it suggests the three times, or tenses of the verb last named; and that it expresses, therefore, God's existence and His eternity.[1] For rea-

---

[1] See Drach's *De l'Harmonie entre l'Eglise et la Synagogue,* Vol. I, pp. 319, 438, 500, 502. Also, *Dictionary of the Bible* (Hasting's), Vol. XXII, p. 199.

sons, not necessary to be detailed here, this impresses the writer as being a superficial, or exoteric explanation, if explanation it be at all, and one which does not, in any event, debar us from pushing further in order to discover whether there be or be not another and a deeper esoteric meaning.

406. If it can be shown that the Tetragrammaton contains in itself, in its very construction, an intimation of the Trinity, an indication of the existence of the Father, the Son and the Holy Ghost, all in one God, the case is changed immediately. If such a proposition can be established, we have a full and fitting explanation for the reserved and reverent attitude of the Jews, so long persevered in, toward the ineffable name.

407. The Hebrew language was written originally in consonants only; and the reader, as he went along, himself supplied the vowel sounds. Therefore, the earlier ages, the divine name, Jehova, was written with four of what we call consonants: *Yod, Hay, Vav, Hay.* These four letters may be represented in English form, thus JHVH.

408. At first blush it seems a strange proposition to advance that the nature of the triune God is represented by a word of four letters and not by one of three only. More careful examination, however, shows that the Tetragrammaton, as thus originally written, contains only three different consonants; there being a repetition, in the fourth place, of the second letter, *Hay.*

409. This is a striking feature of the incommunicable Name, in the shape in which it was first

given to the Jews, that calls for careful study. In fact, from the viewpoint solely of construction, and independently of the question of etymological derivation, this is the only characteristic of the Tetragrammaton which challenges attention. The dogma of the Holy Trinity affords a ready and an intelligible explanation here; and it supplies a reason sufficient for the profound veneration so long accorded by the Jews to this particular Name of God, and its exclusion from profane and popular use.

410. Accepting this key, we are able to unlock the mystery of the Tetragrammaton as follows: *JHVH*, one name, signifying the Unity of God; the J, however, standing for God the Father; the *H*, for God the Son, as to His Divinity; *V*, for the Holy Ghost; and the *H*, repeated and final, joined to the preceding letters and indicating the Sacred Humanity of the Son, united as that Sacred Humanity now is, hypostatically, with the Divine and Eternal Word.

411. It will not be denied that this solution is plausible; and, in absence of a better one, a plausible explanation is always a probable one.

412. But the sufficiency of this solution is put at issue, and it is useful to consider what is the standpoint from which it should be approached and what is the character of the proofs which opponents are entitled to demand from those who advocate it.

413. The facts, which we are to account for, have already been detailed in this chapter, and they relate to the deep and enduring reverence and reserve in which the incommunicable name was held by the ancient Jews. For this, the fair-minded historian

must, as we have seen, seek some just and intelligible motive rather than charge it, off-hand, to stupidity or to superstitition.

414. We are not at this moment concerned with the truth or untruth of the dogma itself of the Holy Trinity. Our only concern now is to know whether the Ancient Hebrews, or at least the wiser ones among them, were acquainted with it and considered that it found expression, or intimation, in the four letters of the Tetragrammaton.

415. No impartial student of history will be influenced or biased, in a study of this sort, by his own religious convictions, or lack thereof, when, as here, he is seeking the origin or cause of a striking religious observance, that has long and universally prevailed among the most ancient human race, or people, still existing.

416. Upon the one real issue before us, there is little extrinsic evidence accessible, except it come from Jewish writings, whose date is subsequent to the birth of Christ.[1] It was only after the Crucifixion, and after the final dispersion of Israel, that

---

[1] We have only a very small volume of really ancient literature from the Hebrews; the Old Testament, and, as close to the border line, Philo and Josephus. But Philo and Josephus wrote for Gentiles rather than for Jews, and neither of them would publish to the unbelieving world the most sacred religious secret of their nation. Under the Old Law of Israel the true significance of the Tetragrammaton cannot have been proclaimed in the streets and roadways, but it was doubtless handed down from generation to generation among the Ancients or Elders. The great care taken to prevent even the utterance of the ineffable name before the Gentiles, or by the Jewish commonalty should satisfy us that its mystic sense, if it had any, would be held in even stricter reserve than the name itself.

the prohibition against the writing down of the oral law was removed, and that the Talmud began to make its appearance.

417. The cardinal fact that the name Jehova was held in reverence and reserve among their people was known, of course, to the Rabbinical writers; and some, at least, among them must have known all of the most hidden mysteries of the old Jewish Faith. But these men, impelled by animosity toward Christ and His Church, antagonized the great truths of the Messiahship and of the divinity of the Lord Jesus; and to that end they felt compelled to combat, also, openly at least, the dogma of the Trinity. Naturally, therefore, the majority of the Rabbins were prompted to suppress, as far as possible, all that might be construed as favoring Christianity.

418. But every rule has its exceptions; and, as there has been a great number of these Rabbinical writers and commentators, since the Crucifixion, it was to be expected that some among them would depart from the traditions of their order, in this regard. And, in several instances, such departures have been made in Rabbinical literature, and in relation to more than one important religious question. These variations from rule, in this connection, are owing, it may be, to inadvertence on the part of particular Rabbins, or to the confidence of some that what they were writing would never come to Christian notice; or, in some cases, loyalty to the truth may have been the cause.

419. Whatever motive there may have been in each case, the admissions in this connection, from the

more candid Rabbis, are in the nature of admissions against interest, and have great value as evidence. And, with regard to the mystic meaning of the Tetragrammaton, with which we are at this moment particularly concerned, if some modern Jewish authors are found admitting the truth, their testimony should prevail over the polemical denials of their fellows, however numerous these denials may be.

420.   R. Solomon Laniado, in his Commentary on Isaiah, under the title *Keli-paz*, says: "The palms, which are taken on the feast of the tabernacles, are as a sign of our victory, of our deliverance from sin and from the power of Samaël, the demon. Since the Children of Israel march with assurance, holding this weapon in hand, it is a sign that they have gained their cause before the tribunal of God, and that they have been purified on the day of expiations. For *the Just*, Master of the World, is *the Just* of whom it is said: '*And the just is the foundation of the world*' (Prov. 10:25). And the remission of sins, which takes place on the day of expiations, by means of the five mortifications which figure [1] *the first hay of the divine* name; letter which stands for *the time to come*,[2] the remission of sins, I say, is prudence."

421.   The Talmud, Treatise *Menahhot*, fol. 29, verso, teaches that the world was created by the letter *Hay*. Thikkune Zohar, on the verse Gen. 1:26,

---

[1] Hay which is the second and the fourth letter of the Tetragrammaton is the fifth letter of the Hebrew Alphabet and stands for the numeral five for which reason it is held, as above, to be figured by the five mortifications, practiced in connection with the day of expiations, rigorous fasting, etc.

[2] Meaning the time of the Messiah.

has the following: "Let us make man. To whom did he address himself in say this? It is certain that it is the *Yod, Hay, Vav, Hay.*"

422. The text of the *Sepher-Zetzira*, Chap. 1, Mischna 1, contains these words: "By the thirty-two admirable ways Jehova has graven His name in the three numerations." On this R. Abraham-ben-David comments: "All these ways are included in the numerations, which are the three names of the Divinity: *Ehye, Yehova, Adonai.* And these ways are found similarly all in the triple numeration . . . in the letters of the blessed name, which are *yod, hay, vav,* and answer to *conception, conceiving, conceived,* the same as to *knowledge, knowing, known.*" R. Moise Nachmenides, in his commentary on the same, speaks of "*yod, hay, vav,* these three letters of the name, *in which all is included.*"

423. *Medrasch-Ruth,* of the *Zohar* on Genesis, fol. 15, col. 61: "The Most Holy, blessed be He, has created in man the name Jehova, which is His proper holy name. The *Yod* is the soul of the soul; this letter is named Adam. Its light extends into three lights, holding to yod. It is, nevertheless, one single light, without any division.

"The *Hay* is named divine soul. It is united with *Yod,* and it extends itself in several rays; and, nevertheless, it is one; that is to say *Yod, Hay,* without division. And God created man to his own image, to the image of God He created him. He created them male and female. The *Vav* is named *Spirit.* It

---

[1] "Et in Spiritum Sanctum, Dominum et Vivificantem, Qui ex Patre, Filioque, procedit."

is qualified, son of *Yod, Hay.*[1] The (second) *Hay*
is named human soul. It is called, also, *daughter.*
Thus there is *Father, Mother, Son, Daughter.*[1]

424. The interpretation, which sees in the two
Hays of the ineffable name, indication of the two
natures of the Eternal Word, divine and human, and
the reference, also, in the passage just quoted, to the
creation of man and the establishment of the human
family, are borne out by the following extract from
Thikkune-Zohar, fol. 12, recto, of the edition of
Thessalonica: "The faithful Shepherd [2] has two faces
(two natures), one celestial, the other terrestrial.
This is why it is written: 'And God created man to
His image, to the image of God.' 'To His image,'
this is the image from above. 'To the image of
God,' this is the image of here below."

425. The *Medrasch-Ruth* of *Zohar-Hhadasch,*
fol. 59, col. 1, is of similar tenor: "The Most High,
blessed be He, created man in the world, and placed
in him His name Jehova; to wit, *Yod,* soul of the
soul; *Hay,* soul; *Vav,* spirit; *Hay* (second), human
soul. He has loaned them these denominations:
Yod, Hay, Father and Mother; *Vav, Hay,* Son and
Daughter."

426. The same, fol. 65, col. 3, reads thus: "Come
and consider that, as there are in man the four let-

---

[1] Showing the entire human family, which, as well as the individual man, is to the image of God. Ascending from the
image to the divine Original, we have referred to here, the
Father, the Word, the Holy Spirit and the Word Incarnate.

[2] The reader will recall here John 10:14: "I am the Good
Shepherd," etc.

ters of Jehova, they are also *in the essence of God.*
Such are the four sacred letters that are named
Adam, and concerning which Holy Scripture says:
'And God created man (Haadam) to his own image.'
From *Yod* results the fear of the Lord of Lords; I
mean that man should fear him. From *Hay* results
reconciliation of man. From *Vav* results for man
fidelity to the holy law. From *Hay* (second) results
meritorious works and removal of sin."

427. The Zohar, on Exodus, fol. 59, col. 236,
explaining Deut. 6:4, speaks of the *four keys,* represented by the four letters of the name Jehova, and
after saying that the *fourth key,* represented by the
second Hay, fourth letter of the Name, had been
placed in reserve under the tree of life, adds: "These
three keys, which are figured by these three letters
become *one.* When they have become one, this last
key rises up and joins itself to this union of triplic-
ity. Jehova, it is He who is represented by the Yod,
 י, first celestial principle of the holy Name. Elohenu, this is the mystery represented by the *heavenly*
Hay, ה, second letter of the name Jehova. Jehova,
this is the emanation which descends to earth, by the
mystery which the letter *Vav,* ו, represents. These
three are of a unity which is unique."

428. Other quotations to similar effect as those
above, coming from Jewish sources, might be added.
Those given, with others, of similar import, may be
found in Chevalier Drach's work, *De l'Harmonie
entre l'Eglise et la Synagogue.* They prove, and
this from Hebrew sources, that there is, in the name
Jehova, some deep and mystical meaning, and they

afford, also evidence, going to show that the same most sacred name did and does indicate to the initiated, the triune nature of God.

CHAPTER XIII.

THE LETTER SCHIN, ON THE JEWISH PHYLACTERIES.

429. IN JEWISH literature, and in some of the Jewish religious practices, evidences are to be found going to show that the wise and holy ones of ancient Israel recognized the dogma of the Trinity. For instance, students of Hebrew history know the deep reverence and close reserve in which the incommunicable name, Jehova, was held in olden Judea, and in which it is, for that matter, still held among orthodox Jews. It is likewise known that some of the Rabbinical writers, explaining this reverence for one particular form of the divine name, and the rigid reserve in which that one form was kept, do so in such way as to indicate that the sacredness of the Tetragrammaton (JHVH) was due to the fact that, by its construction, this name shows God's nature: the J standing for the Father, the first H for the Son, as to His Divinity, the V for the Holy Ghost, and the second H for the Humanity of the Son, hypostatically united with Divinity, in the person of the Messiah.

430. Closely related to the explanation, just noticed, concerning the Jewish attitude toward the Tetragrammaton, as indicating an ancient belief in the Trinity, we have the reverence of Hebrews for the three-headed letter *Schin*, shaped thus, שׁ, and its recognition as an emblem of the Divinity.

431. To this day, orthodox Jews still make use, on stated occasions, of the phylacteries, to which our Lord refers in his arraignment of the Pharisees, as recorded in Chap. 23, verse 5, of Saint Matthew's Gospel. "And all their works they do for to be seen by men. For they make their phylacteries broad and enlarge their fringes."

Hebrew authorities date the use of phylacteries, among the Children of Israel, from the time of Moses; and there is nothing in the custom itself that antagonizes this statement. But critics in this day refuse to credit the traditions of Israel in this regard. They pretend that the scriptural passages relied upon by the Jews, in this connection, were none of them originally intended to be read literally; that, in the beginning, they were all taken only figuratively.[1]

432. Waiving discussion at this moment of Exod. 13:1 to 10, and same 13:11 to 16, we find in Deut. 6:4 to 9, *both senses*, figurative and literal, employed in the same text. Verse 6 of the passage last referred to reads: "These words which I have commanded you, *shall be in your heart*." And verse

---

[1] Did this false interpretation of the text in question arise before the phylacteries came into use? If so, what, long centuries after the death of Moses, was to persuade the Jews generally to a new reading of old texts, which reading was directly against the traditions of their Fathers? What was to convince them universally that, during so many generations, all Israel had been living in disobedience to certain positive injunctions of God? Were the phylacteries first introduced and did, after that, this new interpretation of an old law come into vogue? If so, what originally suggested the novelty, and what brought it into universal favor? And where is any record of the change?

7 carries still further and makes more emphatic and clear the solemn injunction to reverently remember the divine words: "And thou shalt tell them to thy children, and thou shalt meditate upon them sitting in the house and walking on thy journey, sleeping and rising."

433.   After such reiterated and literal commands to keep the words of God *in mind and heart*, are we at liberty to turn verse 8 from its plain literal meaning to one merely figurative, unnecessary, and, when used in that sense, tautological?   The words of this verse 8 are these: "And thou shalt bind them *as a sign* on thy hand, and they shall be and move between thy eyes."   If these words, last quoted, be figurative only, and tautological, must we not take in the same way verse 9: "And thou shalt write them in the entry and on the doors of thy house"?

434.   Passing to Deut. 11:13 to 21, we have, in verse 18, a positive command *to do both things; i. e.*, to keep the sacred words in memory and, also, to place them on hand and forehead.   "Lay up" is the text, "these my words in your minds and hearts, and hang them as a sign on your hands, and place them before your eyes."   Is this not a strange way of construing; to hold that, where one and the same passage enjoins two actions, one internal, and the other external *and as a sign*, that both injunctions relate exclusively to the internal action, and not at all to any external one?

435.   The argument that the Kairite Jews take the texts under discussion, all as figurative is futile. These Sectaries not only rejected the phylactery,

they cast away likewise all the traditions of their race.[1] Being heretical, they differed, of course, from the orthodox; such difference was the essential of the Sect's existence. To show what they held, or did not hold, is not to prove in any way what orthodox Judaism held or did not hold in the earlier ages.

436. But, be it as it may, with regard to the time when this custom of wearing phylacteries was first introduced among the Hebrews, certain it is that these religious appendages were in use in Israel long before the dawn of our modern era. Therefore, if there be anything inscribed upon, or contained within them, which in any way indicates what was the Jewish belief as to the nature of God, such indication comes to us, necessarily, from ancient Judaism.

437. These phylacteries are of two kinds, one worn on the arm and the other on the forehead. We are concerned, at this time, only with the head phylactery, or frontlet, and to it therefore we will confine our remarks. Properly speaking, these phylacteries are slips of parchment, with certain texts of Holy Scripture inscribed upon them; the box and the straps being only contrivances to hold the inscribed parchment in place. The particular texts, thus made use of, are Exod. 13:1 to 10; Exod. 13:11 to 16; Deut. 6:4 to 9; Deut. 11:13 to 21. These parchments are set in such an order that, when the frontlet is in place, the words of God, contained in the verses already referred to, should be before the wearer's eyes, in a literal compliance with Exod.

[1] Milman's *History of the Jews,* Vol. III, p. 135.

13:9; Exod. 13:16; Deut. 6:8, and Deut. 11:18.[1]

438.   The head phylactery, however, shows more than the simple words of God, taken from Holy Scripture, as shown above.   On two sides, or ends of the box or case, right and left, is impressed the mystic letter *Schin*.   And a striking peculiarity here is that the two *Schins* are not written alike; one is the normal *Schin*, with three points or heads, and the other an abnormal one, showing *four heads*.

439.   There must have been some mystic meaning in the placing at all of this particular three-headed letter *Schin*, together with certain selected words of God, before the eyes of believing Jews; and a mystic meaning also, in its duplication and location in the dual situation in which it is found.   Finally, the use of the *Schin*, with four heads, must have also had its own sacred significance.   What satisfactory explanation have we for all this, if it be not that the twenty-second letter of the Hebrew alphabet stands here for the name of God, thus given a position of honor on the Hebrew phylacteries; placed as it were on the brow of Israel, and kept before the eyes of Israel's children?   The explanation which attempts to use the knots in the leather straps holding the two phylacteries in place, in order to spell out the divine name *Shaddai* (Almighty) is open to serious objections.[2]

[1] "Lay up these words in your hearts and minds, and hang them for a sign on your hands and place them between your eyes," Deut. 11:18.   See, also, Exod., 13:16.   Exod. 13:9 and Deut. 6:8 have "before thy eyes," instead of "between your eyes."

[2] "The head phylactery is fitted to the wearer's head by hav-

440. It is, as we have seen, the writings and inscriptions which form the phylactery, properly such; and the straps are mere accessories to hold these texts and inscriptions in place. Further, the purpose of the head phylactery is to hold what is written or impressed "before" or "between" the eyes; and the knot in that strap, supposed to represent the letter daleth, is behind the head and not in front of the wearer's eyes. It would seem that, if the name of God, or any sign or symbol of Him, must appear at all upon, or in connection with the Jewish frontlet, such name in its entirety, or such sign or symbol was as well entitled, as were the scriptural verses already cited, to the place of distinction and honor; that is, before the very eyes of the wearer.

441. The Hebrew word *Shaddai* is composed really of four letters, the *dalet*, or D, being doubled, or repeated. It is, however, in this word written only once, but with a strong *daghesh*, which doubles it. If, therefore, the explanation we are now considering be correct, or exclusive, we might account for a duplication, in some way, of the *dalet* in or on the phylacteries or in the knotting of their straps. Here, however, we have no reproduction of the *dalet*, which would be comprehensible; but it is the *Schin* which is

ing its strap tied at the back of the head into a knot of the shape of *daleth,* ד. One end of the other strap, after being passed through the flap of its phylactery, is formed into a noose, by means of a knot, of the shape of *yod,* י. The schin of the head phylactery, together with these knots thus make up the letters of the sacred name Shaddai, to which a mystical significance is attached." Hasting's *Dictionary of the Bible,* Vol. III, p. 870.

duplicated, without any sufficient justification from the standpoint to which we are now objecting.[1]

442.   If it be conceded that the two *schins*, on the box of the head phylactery, stand as signs or symbols of the Almighty God, by themselves and independent of any knots in tying straps, these signs or symbols are where they should be, in the places of greatest importance and honor; and the duplication of the letter now in question can be readily understood, on the theory that, by so doing, the sacred mark was placed before, as it were, each eye, the right and the left, of every wearer.

443.   It is conceded that "a mystical significance is attached" to the placing of the letter *Schin*, where and as it appears on the Jewish frontlet;[2] but if these letters, with the two knots in the fastening straps, stand for *Shaddai*, where is the place here for any "mystical signification"? Whatever be its derivation, or whatever be the aspect in which it presents God to us, this form of the divine name (Shaddai) is not pretended to be indicative, in any

[1] It may be suggested that the imprinting of the Schin, once on each end of the case or box, was with the idea of balancing, as it were; so as to avoid having a letter on one end only, and a blank on the other. But an objection of this sort would itself suggest another and a more appropriate remedy; the putting of the *schin* upon one end of the case and of *dalet* and *yod* (both of these being narrow letters) on the other. Thus would have been avoided a clumsy device; the spelling of one of the divine names, by the means, in greater part, of straps, or rather knots, and the splitting up, as it were, of the sacred name, and the distribution of its letters between the two phylacteries.

[2] "Together with the knots; all spelling, as it is contended, the name of Shaddai. See Hasting's *Dictionary of the Bible*, Vol. III, p. 870.

especial manner, of the nature itself of the Divinity. And, if this method of presenting *Shaddai*, one part in an actual letter and two parts in a sort of dumb show, be significative of any particular mystery, it is a mystery absolute in its character, and one concerning which even the Ancients of Israel seem to have known little or nothing.

444. Finally, the attempted explanation under consideration is fatally defective, for the further reason that it does not pretend to account for the fourth head or prong which is given to the letter *Schin* when placed upon the left outer wall of the *bayith*, or case, of the Hebrew frontlet.

445. If, on the other hand, it be granted that, among the olden Jews, the Ancients, or Elders, at least knew and accepted the dogma of the Holy Trinity, there is a clear explanation for all which otherwise appears to us inexplicable, in connection with the appearance of the two *Schins* upon the head phylacteries.

446. The letter Schin may be considered as constituted of three *yods*, united into one letter, by a band or bar at the bottom. Now, the letter *yod* has been always considered as a sign or symbol of the Deity. It is closely related to *yodu*, which means "let them praise," or "give glory to." [1] The *Zohar* on Exodus, fol. 59, col. 236, dealing with Deut. 6:4, refers to the *four keys* represented by the *four letters* of the Tetragrammaton, and explains them, de-

---

[1] See Hebrew text of Psa. 107 (Vulgate 106):8, 15, 21, 31; also Psa. 140 (Vulgate 139):14. Drach, *De l'Harmonie entre l'Eglise et la Synagogue,* Vol. I, p. 386.

claring, among other things, "Jehova, this is what is represented by the Yod, ‫י‬, first celestial principle [1] of the holy name."

447.   The Zohar often makes mention of *the three yods of the sacred name*.[2]   In ancient manuscripts of the Targums, the name Jehova is replaced by three points or three yods, underwritten with the vowel Kametz,[3] the said vowel being practically three points, or ends joined by lines, one cross and one perpendicular.

448.   In the Hebrew prayer books of the present time, the ineffable name is still represented by *two* yod, with the kametz below; the third yod having been suppressed when Christians began in some numbers the study of Jewish literature.

449.   If *yod* be recognized as a symbol or sign of God, then a letter which is constituted of three yod, joined together, or which gives the appearance of having been so constituted, is very suggestive of the Holy Trinity; [4] and when we see that letter, thus peculiarly shaped, placed, from a remote antiquity and for some sacred and mystical purpose, upon the brow and before the eyes, bodily and spir-

---

[1] As first letter of the Tetragrammaton.

[2] Drach, *De l'Harmonie entre l'Eglise et la Synagogue,* Vol. I, p. 309; Kircher, *Œdipus Ægypt,* Vol. II, pp. 114, 115; Gerald Massey, *A Book of Beginnings,* Vol. II, p. 153.

[3] Buxtorfii: Dissert. de Nominibus Dei Hebr., No. 28.

[4] It is possible that the Hebrew alphabet developed out of the Ancient Egyptian writing; but we have nothing now to do with this question of ultimate origin.   Our aim is to show that the Hebrew letter *schin* was regarded among the Ancient Jews as a symbol of divinity; and it matters not to us, in this present study, at what particular period the olden Jews came to hold that letter as thus significant.

itual, of every Jew, we may, not unreasonably, conclude that this letter was so employed and so reverenced, because it symbolized the Triune God.[1]

450. From the standpoint of faith in the dogma of the Holy Trinity, we are able to advance a satisfactory explanation for the appearance of two *schins* upon every Jewish frontlet; and, we are able furthermore to solve an otherwise inexplicable mystery, the addition of a fourth yod, or head, to one of the *Schins* so used. The one normal *Schin*, with its three in one appearance, stands for the Trinity, strictly such; the *Schin* of four yods represents the Trinity, with Christ's sacred Humanity hypostatically united to His Divinity.

451. This interpretation finds strong support in the explanation given by some of the Tetragrammaton; the ineffable name of four letters, so particularly reverenced among the Jews, and kept by them in such rigid reserve—JHV standing for the three Divine Persons; and the H repeated, last letter of the Incommunicable Name, representing the Savior's Sacred Humanity. P. B. L. Drach proves that this way of accounting for the two Schins that are placed on the head phylacteries of Israel, is not without support in Rabbinical authority.

452. "The phylactery of the head," writes this author,[2] "bears on one side a *schin*, 𝒲, with three heads, and, on the opposite side, the same letter, with four heads. In the *Zohar*, third part, fol. 126,

---

[1] We are here reminded of the use made by Saint Patrick of the Irish trefoil, or shamrock, to illustrate the Trinity.

[2] *De l'Harmonie entre l'Eglise et la Synagogue,* Vol. I, p. 405.

col. 501, a tradition is reported from Rabbi Isaac, according to which these two forms of the letter indicate the mystery of the Trinity and the mystery of the four letters of the Tetragrammaton.

"The *Zohar* on Genesis, fol. 40, col. 59, teaches that the *Schin,* שׁ, of the name, שׁת,[1] indicates the three branches of the *tree on high,* branches which it reunites, *below,* on the earth, *in one single root.* 'It shows,' the Zohar adds, 'three spheres above and three spheres below. The Hay by which it (*schin*) is followed immediately in the name of Moses, משׁה, is *the divinity of below.* This last letter is repeated twice,[2] to the end that the Hay of above and the Hay of below may be comprised in the three branches[3] and in the triple root.'

"It is thus that we read, also, in the Cabalistic book Schaare Ora (the Gates of Light), fol. 1: 'The name of four letters is like the branches. The name *Ehyé* is the root of the tree. There come forth many roots, which push branches in all directions.' "[4]

---

[1] "*Seth, Son of Adam,* who replaced Abel. Gen. 14:25."

[2] "The name of Moses being repeated twice in verse 4 of Exodus 3."

[3] Right, left and middle.

[4] Right, left and upward. The phylacteries suggest the "fringes"; both being mentioned together by our Lord in Matt. 23:5. The wearing of "fringes" was divinely enjoined. Num. 15:38; Deut. 22:12. Without doubt the fringes here referred to mean "twisted cords." One of these twisted cords is placed at each corner of the mantle; and each "cord" is made up of four threads twisted together. In olden times, one of these threads was blue; later, all of them were allowed to be white, one, however, longer than the other three and called the *shammesh* or "servant." That these fringes had some mystical meaning is undeniable. May not the four cords, at the four corners, and again the four threads united in one cord, be re-

453. The Jesuit Fathers found, among the Jews of China, a similar mysterious signification given to the letters *schin* and *hay*, as related in the "Memoires sur les Juifs, Establis en Chine." Therein it is stated that, in the presence of Fathers Gaubil, Couteaux and Jacques, several Chinese Jews, having been asked concerning the Hebrew word *Schilo*, one of their number spoke, the others present remaining silent. "He said," it is declared in this report, "that one of his grand-uncles, who had been dead some time, had assured him that there was in this word something divine. That the *schin* signified *great*, the *yod*, one, the *lamed*, ל, *who descends*, the *hay*, man."

454. As the colony of Jews in China has been long established in that country, their traditions are entitled to some consideration, as going to show the religious convictions which their distant ancestors brought away with them from the Judean Fatherland.

garded as teaching the same lesson as does the Tetragrammaton, with its four consonants, and the *schin* of four heads, impressed upon the frontlet?

CHAPTER XIV.

The Songs of the Degrees.

455. Fifteen Psalms, from 119 (120) to 133 (134), both inclusive, are grouped together in the Old Testament, and to each of them is given a similar title, one difficult to be explained. In the Douay Translation, this title reads "A Gradual Canticle;" in the Revised Version, "A Song of Ascents," and in the King James Edition, "A Song of Degrees." Isaac Leeser (Jew) translates it, in his version, "A Song of the Degrees." [1]

456. It is not a satisfactory translation of "Canticum Graduum," as found in the Vulgate, to give us, in English, the heading here "A Gradual Canticle;" and there is nothing gained by changing "degrees" into "Ascents," as has been done in the Revised Version. The word "degree" does not necessarily suggest either ascent or descent.

457. Many students have suggested explanations as to the true significance of this title, but it cannot be said that any of these explanations are fully acceptable.

458. Some consider these fifteen canticles as constituting together "A Song of the Return," marking as such, or commemorating, the return or "Ascent"

---

[1] Leeser is here the most accurate, in so far, at least, as that he retains the definite article "the," omitted in other English versions, shown above, but present in the original Hebrew: *Shir hammaalôth.*

from Babylon. I Esdras (Ezra) 7:6, does say that the Prophet "went up from Babylon," and in the same book and chapter (verse 9) is the expression, also, "he began to go up from Babylon."

459. If the return from Babylon be regarded as historically but one single movement, there is no satisfactory reason why the plural form should be used here, "degrees" or "ascents." The striking and impressive fact, in this connection, was the restoration of the Chosen People to the Land of their Forefathers, the Land of Promise. Whether the Children of Israel, on that happy occasion, did their homecoming in one body, practically, or in several detachments, was a secondary matter, scarcely worthy of being shown or represented in the fifteen captions now under consideration. Indeed, it was the nation as a whole [1] which was making this return from captivity, and it would not have been strictly accurate to designate the movements as "returns" or "ascents," simply because the people had found it more convenient to make the home journey in several different bodies.

460. Reversing the picture, it is certain that the Jews were brought to Babylon in more than one deportation, but this fact did not lead to the naming of the great calamity itself as "the captivities."

461. The Psalms themselves, now in question, make no particular mention of the Babylonian exile, and, with a possible exception of 119 (120) and 125 (126), indicate on their faces no intent to associate

---

[1] Of course, we exclude here those who preferred to remain permanently in Babylon.

them, in a special way, with any exile whatsoever. The reference in Psa. 119 (120):5 to the prolonging of some sojourn, and to a dwelling with the inhabitants of Cedar, or Kedar, does not deal apparently with any national experience, but refers to some individual experience of him who composed the song or for whom it was composed. It may be difficult to locate precisely the Cedar, or Kedar, mentioned in the Psalm last referred to, but certainly it is not Babylon.[1] And Psalm 125 (126) does not necessarily refer to the Babylonian deportation. The "captivity" of a nation need not involve the carrying away of its citizens. A people reduced to utter subjection are captives, even though they may be permitted to continue inhabiting the land of their birth.[2] And to "bring back" may be interpreted as restoring affairs to an original happier condition.[3]

462.   The Psalm itself 125 (126), seems to indicate that the particular captivity therein mentioned was, at the time of the first singing of this song, a thing of the past. "When the Lord," it says, "*brought back* the captivity of Zion, *then we became* like men *comforted.*" If this interpretation be correct, the Psalm in question could not well have been "A Song of the Return" from Babylon; that is, a song to be chanted by the Jews when returning from Babylon. If it must be referred to some actual exile this canticle probably deals with the first captivity

---

[1] See Isa. 21:16, 17; same 42:11; same 60:7.

[2] "And bringing into captivity every understanding unto God." II Cor. 10:5.

[3] Thirtle, *Old Testament Problems,* p. 45.

of Israel in Egypt, in which event, as the Psalm was composed long after the Exodus, it could not have been, in any sense, "A Song of the Return."

463. The manifest purpose of this canticle, in any event, is not so much to commemorate a release from captivity as it is, on the strength of such release, to praise and glorify the Almighty,[1] and, at the same time, to inculcate beautiful lessons of confidence in the Divine goodness.[2]

464. The theory is also vulnerable, which holds that these particular Psalms were sung during the pilgrimages to Jerusalem, and that the "degrees" of the captions in question refer to stations at which the caravans halted, on their way to the Holy City. There are one hundred and fifty Psalms in our entire Psalter. Fifteen only are designated as "Songs of the Degrees;" one hundred and thirty-five are not so designated. The interpretation with which we are now dealing, means, therefore, that one only out of every ten of the Psalms was chosen for special use by Pilgrims journeying toward Jerusalem. If this be so, we must search for the principle upon which this selection was based, seek to know why these particular fifteen Psalms were found more suitable for this purpose than the one hundred and thirty-five which were not similarly employed. But, inquiries of this sort meet with no satisfactory response.

465. From the standpoint of the two theories, in

[1] "The Lord hath done great things for them. The Lord has done great things for us," etc. Verses 3, 4.

[2] "They that sow in tears shall reap in joy," etc. Verses 5, *et seq.*

this connection, already touched upon, there was no occasion here for mystification of any sort; no reason why what was meant should not be plainly stated. Consequently, if these fifteen Psalms were so many "Songs of the Return," or so many "Songs for the Pilgrimages," there was no sensible excuse, in either case, for puzzling the faithful, to say nothing of modern Exegetical students, with headings, so obscure as are "Songs of the Degrees," or "Songs of the Ascents."

466. An explanation is attempted to the effect that these headlines are descriptive of the poetical structure of the Psalms; and those who favor this view seek to rest this hypothesis upon a supposed step-like movement, which, it is claimed, may be observed in rhetorical construction of these canticles.[1] It is very questionable, whether this theory suggests an adequate motive for the arrangement we are considering. Could the thought that these fifteen canticles are somewhat similar, in their poetical structure, have been alone sufficient to cause their grouping together and the bestowal upon them of the distinctive caption which is common to them all?

467. But, this supposed step-like movement is

---

[1] The fancied "steps" here, consist of the use in some of these Psalms of the rhetorical and poetical figure known as "Anadiplosis," which consists in "the repetition, at the beginning of a line or clause, of the last word or words preceding." An example is: "I have lifted up my eyes to the mountains, *from whence help shall come to me. My help is (or cometh from) the Lord.*" Psa. 120 (121):1, 2. The resemblance of such a poetical structure to "steps" or a "stairway," or to "degrees," or "ascents" is not very apparent.

not to be observed at all in some of these same fifteen Psalms, 127 (128), 129 (130), 131 (132). Therefore, the caption in question, if intended to merely indicate the presence of anadiploses in these songs is of doubtful application to some of them, and is a positive misfit as to others. Furthermore, a similar poetical structure is discovered in canticles that are not numbered among these fifteen: 92 (93), 97 (98). Why were these other Psalms excluded from this particular Psalter, if the secret of its formation was the gathering together of Psalms which are characterized by the repetitions of words or phrases, of the sort we are now considering?

468. A Rabbinical interpretation assumes that these Psalms were named from the fifteen steps which connected the Court of Israel with the Court of the Women, in the Second Temple. It is asserted that the Levites stood upon these steps, on the first day of the Feast of Tabernacles, singing canticles and playing upon musical instruments, while water was being drawn from the Pool of Siloam, etc. This theory has nothing to support it beyond the coincidence that the steps in question and the Songs of the Degrees, are each fifteen in number. It would have been a strange notion; selecting for exclusive commemoration of this sort, in connection with the ceremony of drawing water from the Siloam Pool, the fact or condition that the singing and playing Levites were standing, as they rendered their music, upon a stair flight of fifteen steps. We could understand, in this connection, the choice, as a common caption for Psalms sung on such an occasion of the

phrase "Song for the Drawing of Water," or "Song of the Levites," but why "Song of the Steps?"

469.   Some are of the opinion that the Psalm caption we are considering indicated that the Canticles thus marked were to be sung in higher tones.   But there is no suggestion of a satisfactory reason why these fifteen should be chosen out of the total of one hundred and fifty Psalms for chanting in a higher tone.   Moreover, it is not to be presumed that these Songs were to be sung in a variety of vocal elevations, or that each was to have a pitch of its own; one or the other of which theories we should hold, in order to warrant the use here of the plural "degrees."   And, there were ways for giving plainly this particular direction, if such were here intended, without having to resort to an obscure hint or doubtful intimation.

470.   Raschi, and after him Schiller-Szinessy, suggest as an explanation that these captions indicate the "liftings up" and "going forth" of the heart to God, which the singing of these Canticles occasioned.   There are very many other Psalms in the entire Psalter, which, as well as these fifteen, are calculated to "lift up the heart" and "send it forth" to God.   Other Psalms, also, as well as 120 (121):1, and 122 (123):1, make use of the words "lift up." [1]

471.   Finally, in the matter of theories, in this connection, we will note as briefly as possible the one which seeks to associate these fifteen "songs of the Degrees" in an especial manner with King Ezechias, or Hezekiah.   It is not pretended that this Jewish

[1] Psa. 23 (24):7, 9; 24 (25):1; 85 (86):4; 142 (143):8.

King composed any of these Psalms, for Holy Writ
does not present him to us as the author of Canticles,
and the Psalms in question are historically and tra-
ditionally ascribed to others. Four of them actually
bear the name of David at their head, and one the
name of Solomon.[1]

Did Ezechias collect them together into one group,
and command them to be sung collectively as a commemoration of his own merits and his own exploits?
Holy Scripture is somewhat elaborate in its details,
as to the life and actions of this particular Judean
King. If it be true that he established this Psalter
of fifteen Psalms, and that fact was deemed worthy
of being recorded, why is there no express mention
thereof in those portions of Holy Writ that deal
with his life and doings? Why are we left in this regard to weak and uncertain inferences, which may be
forced, if we are determined to do so, from the vague
and vexing captions which have been given to these
Canticles?

472. It is true that Ezekias, as appears from
Isa. 18:20, made this promise in the event of his
cure: "We will sing our Psalms[2] all the days of our
life, in the House of the Lord." But this is only a
rhetorical way of declaring that, if he were healed,
the King and his people would perseveringly praise

[1] In II Paralipomenon (Chronicles) 29:30, it is said: "And
Ezechias and the Princes commanded the Levites to praise the
Lord, with the words of David and Asaph, the Seer."

[2] This rendition, according to the Vulgate, the Revised Version has it "My Songs," but the difference does not materially
affect the sense. It is not pretended that Ezechias composed
these fifteen Canticles, or that they were in any manner his
exclusive property.

and glorify the Almighty. It cannot mean that Exechias promised, in the event stated, to select fifteen particular canticles, put them together in a special Psalter, and have them sung in commemoration of his own experiences and exploits.

473. If it be that the grouping together of these fifteen sacred songs, and the bestowing upon them of their similar captions, was intended as a perpetual remembrance of Ezechias, the same spirit which inspired the doing, for such a purpose, of this much, would doubtless have suggested the use here of captions which would make plain the purpose existing, and establish a true and unmistakable memorial. As things are, the non-appearance of the name of Ezechias in these captions, the absence of anything in all of Holy Writ to connect him in a particular manner with these Psalms, furnishes a strong argument against the correctness of the particular guess which we have now under consideration.

474. This same hypothesis takes no true support from the fact, related in Holy Scripture, that Ezechias, when about to die, was granted by the Lord a respite of fifteen years; and that, in verification of His promise, in this case, the Lord caused the shadow on the dial of Achaz to move back *ten degrees.* IV (II) Kings 20:6, 9, 10, 11.

475. That there was no special association, or connection, in the divine mind between the "degrees" on the dial and the "years" of added life given to the Jewish King appears from the difference in numbers between the two; of the degrees there were ten, and of the years, fifteen. We may rest assured that a dis-

crepancy of this sort would not have existed here, had it been intended by the Lord that the degrees on the dial, through which the shadow passed back, should be typical of the years of prolonged life given Ezechias. If the similarity in number between the Songs in question, and the added years of life in this case, argues connection between Songs and years, why should not the dissimilarity in number between the years and the degrees of recession on the dial, and between the Songs and the same degrees, tend to establish disconnection?

476. We must recognize the fact that, *per se,* there is no very striking figurative resemblance between the degrees upon a sun dial, or between degrees of any sort, and the years of a human life. Certainly it would have been clearer, from the standpoint of the theory we are now discussing, had these captions read each "A Song of the Years" instead of a "Song of the Degrees," as they are written.

477. In pushing further our search, let us look for some characteristic, if any there be, that is common to these fifteen Psalms. It is not necessary for our purpose, however, that we seek a characteristic which belongs, with absolute exclusiveness to them.

478. James William Thirtle, thus describes, in this regard, this collection of sacred canticles:

"Before proceeding to examine the headline, we may note *the distinct spirituality of the Songs.* What is on the surface of most of them is applicable to each and all. *They are Temple hymns. They were obviously designed for use in the worship of Jehovah,* and their language is that of the Sanctuary.

We read of 'Jerusalem' (122:2, 3, 6; 125:2; 128:5); [1] 'Zion,' 'Mount Zion,' and 'the Mountains of Zion' (125:1; 126:1; 128:5; 129:5; 132:13; 133:3; 134:3); 'the House of the Lord' (122:1, 9; 134:1); 'the Sanctuary' (134:2); 'priests' (132:9, 16). *The Tetragrammaton occurs over fifty times, no single song being without it.*" [2]

479. These Psalms may justly be considered as specially devoted to Jehova, and as specially fitted for the praising and glorifying of Him. Therefore, may we not now wisely search for some particular correspondence between the common title given to each of these fifteen Psalms, on one hand, and the name or nature of the great Jehova on the other?

480. If we approach this problem from the standpoint of the dogma of the Holy Trinity, we can find some correspondence, or connection between the ineffable Name with the intimations as to the Divine nature which that name affords, and our hymn caption. Disabusing our minds of the preconceived notion, if such we unfortunately entertain, that nothing in the Old Testament can by any possibility relate to the Trinity, need we be surprised to find that "Degrees," as the word is used in these captions, refers to the Divine Persons of the Triune God, and that a fair reading of each of these titles is "A Song to (or for or in honor of) the Divine Persons?"

[1] These numberings of Psalms are according to the Revised Version. The Songs thus numbered may be located in the Vulgate and in the Douay Translation thereof, by reducing in each of these references by one the Psalm numbers put down in the above quotation. Thus Psalm 122 of the text is No. 121 of the Vulgate, and so on.

[2] James William Thirtle, *Old Testament Problems,* p. 11.

481. If this be a correct solution, we have reason for the reference here, in a veiled manner only, to the Holy Trinity: for there was an esoteric as well as an exoteric side to the religion of the Ancient Jews. And this mystery, if known among the Ancients of Israel, was such a part of the deposit of faith as would be held in strictest reserve. It would be handed down orally, and when shown at all in the written law, the reference thereto would be more or less veiled.

482. These fifteen Psalms, constituting the Songs of the Degrees, were to be sung publicly in the Temple, therefore, any reference made therein, either in the captions or in the texts, to the deeper mysteries of Religion called for careful cloaking, so that adepts might understand, but not the uninitiated.

483. The word degree may be used to express other ideas than merely one of steps or ascents. Nor does it necessarily imply difference in power or importance or in elevation. Sons and daughters are not necessarily inferior in any way to fathers and mothers; or nephews and nieces to uncles and aunts. Nevertheless these different relationships are properly expressed by the phrase "degrees" of consanguinity.

484. The dogma of the Holy Trinity shows one God, in three Divine Persons; the Father, the Son and the Holy Ghost. The Son, this dogma teaches, was begotten of the Father, eternally; and the Holy Ghost proceeds, also eternally, from the Father and the Son.

485. Typical of this, though upon a plane infi-

nitely lower and serving as an image only, the first woman was from the first man, and from both of them, the child. We may well speak figuratively of the man, the woman and the child as the degrees of the human family; and, there is no reason why the ancient Jews might not similarly have written or spoken figuratively and esoterically of the three Divine Persons, as the Degrees of the Divine Family, the Holy Trinity. In this light, the fifteen Psalms, with each its impressive caption, "A Song of the Degrees," may be fairly held as referring to the three Degrees or Persons who are the one eternal and triune God.

486. Despite the antagonism to the dogma of the Holy Trinity which developed among the unconverted Jews, after the Resurrection, and despite the anxiety which possessed the Rabbins to discountenance all that might favor the Christian teaching of the Savior's divinity, the theory we are now propounding, with regard to the fifteen Psalm captions now in question, is not without some support in the Rabbinical writings. The word "Degrees" is found employed by Jewish Cabalists, as one of the divine names, or if not unmistakably so, certainly the term has been used by them as expressing close relationship, or connection of some sort, with God. Drach tells us: "In the language of the Cabalistic Rabbins, the *three degrees* are the three divine Hypostases," etc.[1]

487. Commenting on Psa. 62 (63):2 (1), the

---

[1] Drach's *De l'Harmonie entre l'Eglise et la Synagogue,* Vol. I, p. 414, footnote (a).

Zohar, Part II, fol. 62, col. 248, explains as follows: "David has sung a praise sublime and eminent; and which is it? *God, my God, Thou.* For, why, after having said *God*, does he repeat *my God*, if this was not to announce *another degree*, which is proper to God? We see in this verse *the three degrees, God, my God, Thou.* Although they are three, it is only one *unique degree* in the mystery of the living God.

"God, God Supreme, God Living, my God, from one extremity of the heaven to the other extremity of the heaven. *Thou*, Degree that is inherent in him. Nevertheless, the *all* is but one, and reduces itself to one only Name." [1]

488. The same cabalistic work, Zohar, on Genesis, fol. 89, col. 350, says: "Jehova held Himself on the ladder of Jacob, because on that ladder all His degrees were seen united in one knot." [2]

489. And the Zohar, also, fol. 30, col. 141, referring to Psalm 109 (110), "The Lord said to my Lord," etc., has the following: "R. Simeon has begun in these terms the exposition of Psalm 110 (109) Jehova said to my Lord. The *Supreme Degree* said to the *Degree* below,[3] sit thou at my right."

490. Part II, fol. 19, col. 74, 75, of same Work: "The first chapter (of Phylacteries), *sanctify* unto

---

[1] Jehova, JHVH, a name symbolizing the Trinity; J standing for God the Father; H for God the Son; V for God the Holy Ghost, and H repeated, for the Humanity of Christ, hypostatically united with the Divinity.

[2] Knot, figuratively representing or suggesting a close and intimate union.

[3] "Degree of below," plainly the Divine Son, made man."

me every first born,[1] is the celestial mystery which
reunites the four cases [2] in the mystery of the celestial light which comes from the '*No.*' [3] The second
chapter, "And it shall be," וְהָיָה, indicate *prudence*
as in this chapter the coming out of Egypt is referred to, which is in the nature of a jubilee; for this
reason it (the second chapter, or phylactery text)
commences with the letters of the Tetragrammaton.[4]
That which shows this mystery is ready to descend
and to light up the lights and *to dwell in the degree
below.*[5]

"This mystery operates in a manner hidden from
the intelligence; for this reason, we do not read it
openly in this name, and it has been confided to the
Sages," etc.

[1] Exod. 13:2.

[2] The Jewish head phylactery, or frontlet, consists of four
small receptacles, or cases, joined together and worn on the
forehead, between or before the eyes. In each of these receptacles is a parchment; and on each parchment is written an
extract from Holy Scripture. The four texts enclosed are
Exod. 12:2, 10. Same, verses 11 to 16; Deut. 6:4-9; same
11:12-20.

[3] In Hebrew, אֵין, expresses negation, also it stands for our
"whence." It is used in the original of the text quoted above
to express the idea that God is inscrutable. A passage from
the Thikkunim of the Zohar, fol. 126, recto. treating of verses
1 and 2, psalm 120 (121), particularly of the words "whence
help shall come to me. My help is from Jehova," assigns this
mystical significance to the Hebrew word now in question:
"Aleph," א, this is the *Supreme Crown;* Yod, י, Wisdom;
Nun, ן, Prudence."

[4] The sacred text included in the boxes of the Hebrew front-
lets are designated, for short, by their opening words. The
passage above referred to begins in Hebrew, thus: וְהָיָה.
It will be observed that we have here the four letters of the
Tetragrammaton, with interversions.

[5] "And the Word was made flesh." John 1:14.